CU00732502

When *Streets and Neuks* was published towards the close of 2000, it was an immediate success. The 2000 copies went like the proverbial *snaw aff a dyke*. Since then, so many people have asked where to obtain a copy that the decision was taken to reprint it. It had been hoped that a lot of new information and some corrections provided by readers could be included, but time has not allowed that. Perhaps at some other time we will be able to produce an expanded version of this book.

Kilmarnock is continuing to grow and many new streets have been added in the last year. In the 1960s Kilmarnock was a boom town that could boast full employment and a host of world beating industries such as Johnnie Walker, BMK, Saxone, Glenfield and Kennedy, Barclays and so on.

The decline of heavy industries hit Kilmarnock hard and for a generation the town has been a depressed area, but things are improving at an accelerating rate. The promise of a new motorway linking Kilmarnock to Glasgow City centre has already attracted huge investment in the top end of the town. Hundreds of new houses have been built in Southcraig and the area around it. New businesses have come in. Firms like The Sandwich Company, an early settler there, have flourished. This new investment is bringing in new people, new vitality and new jobs. It's not restricted to one area. Plans are in hand to revitalise the area around the old infirmary and there are plans for houses at the Mount and for houses and industry around Treesbank. Gap sites are being filled in and in many parts of the town, building work is helping to bring back prosperity to the town.

Like many others, I enjoy looking back with pride at Kilmarnock's past glories. The past is important, for if we ignore the past, we can have no hopes for the future.

Frank Beattie, October 2001.

© 2000 Frank Beattie and the Kilmarnock Standard.

First printed 2000 by Walker & Connell Ltd., Hastings Square, Darvel and published by the Kilmarnock Standard, 1 Bank Place, Kilmarnock, KA1 1HJ.

Reprinted 2001 by Walker & Connell Ltd. and published by Alloway Publishing Ltd., Hastings Square, Darvel, Ayrshire, KA17 0DS.

Other local history books by Frank Beattie:

Kilmarnock in Old Picture Postcards, European Library, 1984
Greetings from Kilmarnock, Stenlake Publishing, 1994

CONDITIONS OF SALE

This book is sold subject to the conditions that it shall not, by way of trade or otherwise, be lent, re-sold, hired out or otherwise circulated without the publisher's prior consent, in any form of binding or cover other than that in which it is published and without a similar condition including this condition being imposed on the subsequent purchaser.

"Streets and Neuks"

When Robert Burns wrote "Tam Samson's Elegy" in 1787 he was writing what was probably correct at that particular time as Kilmarnock had narrow streets which twisted and wound their way around the Cross.

It was when the Duke of Portland became the feudal owner, in 1805 he opened King Street and the road to Riccarton - the straightest road in Auld Killie - took the traffic off Sandbed and gave the town room to expand and accept industry which could be developed and created work for people who lived at that time. An official report 'The Municipal Corporations in Scotland" states "the town of Kilmarnock is the largest in the country, and, by the census of 1831, had a population of 18,093. It is the seat of flourishing manufacturers, and is most particularly noted for the weaving of shawls and carpets. The annual value of these two branches of manufacture is estimated at about £300,000."

In its latter days the last council of the Burgh of Kilmarnock prior to 1975 had to decide how it tackled the modern need for the motor car and drew up plans for containing the traffic. However, the plans agreed by that council never reached fruition, and the formation of the two tier system of Kilmarnock & Loudoun, and Strathclyde Regional Council did not seem to agree, and the road pattern designed with the planners did not materialise. It is my opinion that the present traffic system is the result of the two minds thinking differently, and the great increase in the volume of motor cars puts us in a position which had not been agreed.

It is probably correct that the Kilmarnock Standard should produce a book about the 'Streets & Neuks' of Killie in this millennium year. I was invited to write a short 'lead in' to this book and it gives me much pleasure to do so as a past Provost of Kilmarnock and Loudoun District Council and I hope that all readers have much pleasure in browsing through the streets with me.

Tom Ferguson JP

Past Provost

Kilmarnock & Loudoun District Council.

Acknowledgements

Not long before Burns came to Kilmarnock to persuade John Wilson to print his poems in 1786, Kilmarnock was a large village. There was High Street, Soulis Street, Fore Street, Back Street, Croft Street, Strand Street and the Sandbed. There were a few lanes and tenements, but that was all. Riccarton was a separate village. Netherton was a cluster of cottages and Beansburn was a clachan some distance from the town. The streets and lanes of Kilmarnock were narrow and crooked. Who at that time could have imagined a town stretching from Treesbank to Meiklewood; a town swallowing up Riccarton, Netherton, Beansburn and the farms at the Grange, Altonhill and Wardneuk and stretching from Crosshouse to Crookedholm? Today, Kilmarnock, including Riccarton, has about 700 streets, lanes, drives and avenues. This book takes a look at a selection, in particular those which have been demolished.

I would like to give particular thanks to Alan Woodison, editor of the Kilmarnock Standard who took it on himself to handle all the groundwork required to produce a book; all the boring bits that have nothing to do with searching through old maps and books.

I would also like to give particular thanks to Ann Amor, Tom Ferguson, Norman Gee, John Hall, Alastair MacInnes, Jim Macintyre, Gabrielle McCracken, John McGill and Stuart Wilson for helpful information and Gordon Robb for photographs.

Thanks also go to staff of the Mitchell Library in Glasgow and to staff of South Ayrshire library services at the Carnegie Library in Ayr.

Finally, any comments or indeed any additional information or photographs would be welcomed for publication in the Kilmarnock Standard's weekly Memories page. Write, call or drop in to the Kilmarnock Standard Office in Bank Place and ask for me.

Frank Beattie,

The Burns Monument as presented in a greeting card from 1909.

Academy playing fields

The Kilmarnock Academy Playing Fields at Queen's Drive were opened in 1927. Despite being remote from the school, they have served the school and the town well.

Academy Street

Academy Street in Riccarton at one time led to the parish school of Riccarton. It joins Little Bellsland Road and goes by the former Bellsland Cricket ground. Part of Academy Street was formerly known as Pie Raw.

Aird Avenue

Aird Avenue, off Dundonald Road is probably named after Marion Paul Aird, a 19th century poet and artist who lived in Kilmarnock.

Aitken Street

Aitken Street was close to the Old High Kirk and was named after Rev James Aitken who was minister of that church in the 1870s. He worked relentlessly, particularly for the homeless and destitute children of the town. The street existed into the 1970s. The site is now a car park.

Ales Square

Ales Square is a small open area at the top of the Foregate, named after the town in France which is twinned with Kilmarnock. There is a plaque and a stone giving details of the twinning. There are other town twinning features at Foregate Square and in Howard Park. The Clydesdale Bank here is a rare example of imaginative architecture from the 1970s when much of the old centre of Kilmarnock was demolished and redeveloped.

Alexandra Place

Alexandra Place is one of the red sandstone tenement terraces making up Old Mill Road. The name is still visible, but only just, on the corner of Dick Road and Old Mill Road, opposite Lillymount Place.

Altonhill

Altonhill, sometimes referred to as Altenhill on old maps, was a farm between Kilmarnock and Kilmaurs. It has given its name to a general area of Kilmarnock and to Altonhill Avenue.

Amlaird Road

Amlaird is the name of the water filter plant close to Waterside, two miles from Fenwick. The origin of the name remains obscure.

Annanhill

Annanhill House off the Irvine Road has given its name to a golf course, an Avenue opposite and more recently there has been Annanhill Mews. The mansion house and grounds were bought by the town council in 1929, using profits from the municipal electricity service. Plans to create a golf course started in 1929 but the course was not opened until 1957.

Arbuckle Street

Arbuckle Street is named after a Bailie James Arbuckle, who worked tirelessly for the poor and to see the success of late 19th century soup kitchens. This is a dog legged street linking Glebe Road to Old Mill Road. Most of the houses are traditional red sandstone tenements and some of the even numbered ones were at one time referred to as Symington Terrace.

Ardbeg Avenue

Ardbeg Avenue is set in the midst of a council housing scheme. Here is the Hunter Centre, a fine leisure and community centre named after local councillor John Hunter, Snr.

Armour Street

Armour Street was a street of tenement houses going from Titchfield Street to where Saint Andrew Street meets Gilmour Street. It and Armour Place are named after Stuart Armour, for services to the local community.

Arness Terrace

Arness Street, just off Newlands Drive, takes its name from Arness Farm at Waterside, near Fenwick.

Arrothill Drive

Arrothill is one of the old names that has been used for a modern street name. At the start of the 19th century, Arrothill was a house close to the bank of the River Irvine, between Kilmarnock and Gatehead.

Ascog Avenue

Ascog Avenue was one of the residential streets between Deanhill Road and Hillhead Avenue. It is named after a bay, village and loch on Bute.

Assloss

Assloss House is in the Dean estate close to Dean Castle. There are also Assloss Cottage, Assloss Mains, Assloss Bridge and Assloss Road. The origin of the name remains obscure.

Ava Terrace

Ava Terrace is part of Bonnyton Road, just beyond Munro Avenue. The origin is obscure. Ava was the ancient capital of the Burmese empire. Britain was involved in three wars there in the 19th century, so the name may relate to that.

Ava Terrace, part of Bonnyton Road

Avon Place

Avon Place is named after one of the many small burns which used to flow in the area around Kilmarnock.

Ayr Road

As the name implies Ayr Road is the main road out of Kilmarnock on the way to Ayr. Many of the buildings facing on to it are council houses. An apocryphal story from at least the 1950s and 1960s was that Kilmarnock Town Council would only allow tenants to take houses there if they were good gardeners, so that the route into town gave a good impression to visitors.

Back Causeway

Back Causeway was one of the very old streets in the town centre. For a while in the 1840's it was home to a popular theatre.

Back Lane

Back Lane was once the southern boundary of the town. It was one of the lanes that led off King Street and ran into Braefoot.

Back o' the Yards

The Back o' the Yards was situated at the edge of the gardens of the homes in Back Street and is now called Garden Street.

Back Road

Back Road was an early name for what is now Saint Andrew Street. It lead from the town to the slaughter house, a quarry and Paxton's brewery.

Back Street

Back Street was originally called Smiddie Raw (or Smiddieraw), and as such it was one of the very early streets of the town, probably dating from around the 17th or 18th century. As the earlier name implies it was a lane with several blacksmiths. It marked the North West edge of town. It contained Sandy Patrick's pub, frequented by Burns. This area was redeveloped early in the 19th century to make way for Portland Street.

Balmoral Terrace

Balmoral Terrace was a name sometimes used for part of Henrietta Street.

Bank Place

Bank Place is a short street linking John Finnie Street and Bank Street. A building on the corner of Bank Place and Bank Street, currently used by the Kilmarnock Standard, is dated 1870.

Bank Street

Bank Street was built on the Kirkhaugh, which gently sloped from the Laigh Kirk to the bank of the Kilmarnock Water. The older part of the street was first built on in 1710 on ground that was originally part of the Laigh Kirk burial ground. The sloping ground down to the river was built up to make it level so the new street could be built on it. Many of the old buildings in Bank Street have been able to retain their character. In Bank Street, you will find Stan Reid, a gentleman always absorbed in the Kilmarnock Standard. When a search was launched for ideas for art works for the town centre, children of New Farm Primary School suggested a man reading the Kilmarnock Standard. The Standard he is reading has adverts from the sponsors of the project. When completed the feature was dedicated to the memory of children murdered in Dunblane school in 1996.

Bank Street and the memorial to the Kilmarnock Standard.

Bannockburn Place

Bannockburn Place is named after Bannockburn near Stirling where the Scots defeated English invaders in 1314, thus asserting independence for Scotland. The leader of the Scots was Robert the Bruce, born at Turnberry in Ayrshire.

Barbadoes Road

Barbadoes Road was the road leading to Barbadoes Green but whether or not there is a connection with the island of the same name is no longer certain.

Barbadoes Green

In 1749 the Barbadoes Green and Wards Park were sold to the Earl of Glencairn by the town council. He was the superior of the burgh at that time. The area was between the river and Waterside Street, and part of it was later used for the cattle market. The origin of the name is not known.

Bark Brae

Bark Brae was a feature on the Kilmarnock Water and close to where the railway viaduct crossed the river, there was at one time the Bark Brae Dam.

Barnweil Road

Barnweil Road in Riccarton took its name from Barnweil near Symington. From there Sir William Wallace is said to have looked back at the flames of the barracks of the English soldiers at Ayr after his attack on them.

Bawsey Mountains

The Bawsey Mountains was the curious nickname for an area of open ground on the bank of the River Irvine adjacent to the Academy Playing Field. After the major flood of 1932, much of the area was filled in with slag from the power station.

Bellfield House, now demolished.

Beansburn

The name Beansburn comes from the Beans Burn which flows - or trickles - into the Kilmarnock Water near Tam's Loup. The origin of the name is obscure but a map of 1783 notes it as Beanies Burn. Local legend is that it is named after a girl who drowned herself in one of its pools. Until 1883. Beansburn was 'a little clachan'. In the first half of the 19th century low thatched houses began to be replaced by what was then described as fine villas. It is now part of the main road out of Kilmarnock between Dean Street and Glasgow Road.

Bell o' the Brae

In coaching days the Bell o' the Brae was part of the route through Kilmarnock. By the end of the 19th century only Bellsbrae Cottage remained.

Bellevue Road

Bellevue Road in Bonnyton was first developed for council housing in the 1930s.

Bellfield

Bell is a common prefix for various features in Kilmarnock and includes, Bellsland, Bellsford and Bellfield, but who the Bell of Bellfield or Bellsland was, is uncertain. Bellfield gave its name to a 1960s housing scheme built around what had been Bellfield House and gardens. Part of the gardens remain as woodland and is still a popular walk. Bellfield House and estate was given to the people of the town by the Buchanan family and the estate was opened to the public in 1888.

Bentinck Street during the 1994 flood.

Bellsburn Place

Bellsburn Place is another of the streets with the Bell prefix. The street went off Kirktonholm Street and followed the line of a one time burn which ran past Elmbank House.

Bellsland

Bellsland was a farm to the south of Kilmarnock, but the land was absorbed as the town grew. Today we have Bellsland Place and Little Bellsland Road.

Bentinck Street

Bentinck Street began to be developed in the 1820s and was named after William Henry Cavendish Bentinck, the Duke of Portland. This street was home to Duncan McMillan, who found national acclaim as a ventriloquist and to John Curdie, artist. When Alexander Kay gave money to the town for two schools one of them was built in Bentinck Street. Bentinck Street was extended in 1872 to its junction with East Shaw Street. Before that, what is now James Little Street formed part of Bentinck Street.

Between the Dykes

Between the Dykes was the original name for Mill Lane which was a connecting lane between Mill Road and New Mill Road.

Bickering Bush

Local tradition says that when he was a young man Sir William Wallace was fishing on the banks of the River Irvine, when he was accosted by English soldiers who demanded the fish he had caught. This led to a confrontation which left three of the invaders dead. The Bickering Bush was the name of a thorn bush which was said to have marked the site of the conflict. In later years a pub in Riccarton used the name.

Blackmarys

Blackmarys was a popular name for a gap site in Bentinck Street in the 1950s and early 1960s. The origin of the name is not known.

Black Rock

The Black Rock and a nearby pool known as the Black Pool were features on the Kilmarnock Water at a bend in the river at what is now the Kay Park. The name was used until the 1970s when the pool was filled in to prevent accidental drownings.

Blacksyke Avenue

Blacksyke appears as a feature on old maps on what is now the golf course at Caprington, and is the name of a ruin on the golf course.

Blackwood Avenue

Blackwood Avenue is named after James Blackwood, a Victorian scientist and engineer from Kilmarnock who spent much time studying geology and astronomy, experimenting with electricity and making his own instruments. He was a partner in one of the firms which ultimately merged to form BMK carpets.

Blair Street

Blair Street is probably named after local industrialist Bryce Blair. The first houses were built here in the 1890s.

The Bleachie

In the 1950s and 1960s there was open ground at what was then Paxton Street known as The Bleachie, having been at one time a bleaching green.

Bond Lane

Bond Lane was described by Archibald Adamson in 1875 as 'a vile-looking passage'. It was a lane which is supposed to have led to a whisky bond, though which bond is not known. It was close to Clerk's Lane and the vestry for the Clerk's Lane Church was in Bond Lane.

Bone Lane

Bone Lane was a short lane near the Cross and just off Regent Street, presumably taking its name from one or more butchers shops being there.

Bonfire Knowe

This hill known as Bonfire Knowe in the first half of the 19th century was situated off the Glasgow Road just about where the Dean Park is now.

Bonnyton

A map of the town as it was in 1783 shows Bonnyton, sometimes referred to as Bonnington, as a farm to the west of the town and well away from any built up developments. Today the name is used as a general area of the town. Bonnyton Park was opened in 1909.

Bonnyton Road

As the town grew, it absorbed all the land of Bonnyton farm. Bonnyton became a general term for the area and other parts of the area with the name include Bonnyton Cottages, High Bonnyton Road, Bonnyton Park Road, Bonnyton Place and Bonnyton Square. Some of the rows of red sandstone tenement houses in Bonnyton Road have their own Terrace names such as Kilgour Terrace and Ava Terrace. Between these two is another terrace, but the name is obscured by the ravages of time. The bridge taking the railway across Bonnyton Road has a builders plate on it, but unless the road is exceptionally quiet it is a life threatening process to try to read it.

Bonnyton Square

The houses which formed Bonnyton Square were built by the Glasgow and South Western Railway Company to house their workers. The company moved its main engineering works from Glasgow to Kilmarnock in 1856.

Bouverie Place

Bouverie Place was at Old Irvine Road and was named after local MP Captain E P Bouverie, who was MP for Kilmarnock from 1844 to 1874.

Boyd Street

Boyd Street was described in 1875 as 'a very ancient street, lined on either side with old fashioned houses'. It was originally Mountgean, where gean or wild cherry trees grew. Later it became New Raw, presumably after houses were built there for the first time, then Morris Street. The Boyd family held Dean Castle for several centuries.

Braefoot

There was a fairly steep hill in the middle of London Road, which was cut through by the unemployed in 1826 and again in 1837. Braefoot, Braehead and Braeside are remnants of that steep hill.

Braehead Brae

Braehaed Brae was near Braehead House, just off London Road, behind what is now Henderson Church. Braehead Court is on a hill on one side of it and Kilmarnock Academy is on the other.

Braeside Street 100 years ago.

Braehead Court

Braehead House was a mansion off London Road. After it was demolished, houses were built in the 1960s and took the name of Braehead Court.

Braeside Street

Much of the line of Braeside Street still exists, though most of the buildings have been demolished. Situated just off London Road. On one side was a tenement building, still standing, known at one time as the Maxwell Building and on the other was Tam Samson's home.

Brewery Road

Brewery Road led to one of the town's breweries. This one was that of George Paxton, who is also remembered in Paxton Street. The Brewery was on the banks of the River Irvine.

Bridge End

Before East and West Shaw Streets were built, Bridge End went west from the bridge over the River Irvine at Low Glencairn Street.

Bridge Lane

Bridge Lane is one of several short and narrow lanes leading from King Street to the Sandbed. This one leads to the Timmer Brig and Nelson Street.

Brigade Court

When the fire station was moved from Titchfield Street to Riccarton, the disused building, constructed in 1937, was renovated. The ground floor was converted for commercial use and the firemen's home revamped as flats. The exterior of the building, facing on to Titchfield Street still has the burgh coat of arms and a fireman's helmet worked into the stonework.

Broomhill Quadrant

In the immediate post-war years there was a desperate need for housing and more than 200 temporary homes - 'pre-fabs' - were built in Kilmarnock. Some were later revamped and had brick cladding added. Broomhill Quadrant in Shortlees still had some in 1994, named after the 'Dower House' for Treesbank.

Bruce Street

Bruce Street and Bruce Crescent are named after King Robert the Bruce, who was born at Turnberry and led the Scots to victory at the battle of Bannockburn in 1314. Other streets in this part of Riccarton also relate to Wallace and Bruce.

Buchanan Street

Buchanan Street was named after the Buchanan family who owned Bellfield House and the Bellfield estate. They gave the house to the town for the benefit of the people of Kilmarnock.

Bullet Road

The Bullet Road also sometimes referred to as the Ballot Road, was the northern boundary of the ancient Wards Park. The bullet road is now Dundonald Road. The name comes from the old game of bullets which was commonly played there.

Burnpark Row

Burnpark Row, or Burnpark Cottages was a group of miners' houses on the Ayr Road just about where Townend Road is now.

Burns Avenue

Burns Avenue is named after Robert Burns in commemoration of his many associations with Kilmarnock.

Broomhill Quadrant pre-fabs, 1994.

Burns Mall

The Burns Mall or Burns Shopping Centre was originally called the Burns Precinct but there was so much popular opposition to the use of that term that the name was changed. The centre was built in the 1970s on land that was Duke Street, Waterloo Street and other areas. At the entrance from the Cross there is a stone tablet commemorating the executed Covenanting hero, John Nisbet. In earlier times this stone was set into the roadway near the Cross. Also near the entrance is a plaque marking the site of John Wilson's print shop where the first edition of Burns poetry was printed in 1786. This plaque was originally set up in Waterloo Street.

Burnside Street

Burnside Street takes its name from its proximity to the Kilmarnock Water.

By-Pass

The A77 Kilmarnock by-pass road was built as dual carriageway from Spittalhill to Meiklewood. It was planned from at least the late 1940s but was only built in the early 1970s.

Cairns Terrace

Cairns Terrace is a group of modern houses between Yorke Place and Irvine Road, named after Danny Cairns, one time Provost of Kilmarnock.

Campbell Place

Campbell Place is just off Campbell Street. Here is the former Riccarton School, now a nursery school. The building, dated 1908 has a distinctive and charming architecture.

Quaint architecture in Campbell Place. This 1908 former school is now Riccarton Nursery School

Campbell Street, now home to the fire station.

Campbell Street

Campbell Street forms part of the main route through Riccarton from Kilmarnock to the Ayr Road. It is named after the Campbells of Loudoun. The town's fire station is here and there is a plaque marking the connection with the Wallaces of Riccarton who did so much to ensure Scottish independence.

Cambuskeith

Cambuskeith is an earlier name for the area at the Mount, which at the time was part of the Grange.

Caprington Avenue

Caprington Avenue in Shortlees is named after Caprington Castle. Although much of the castle dates from late 19th century, it is a very old castle. It is said to have belonged to a branch of the Wallace family who obtained a charter for it sometime prior to 1385.

Caprington Close

Caprington Close, sometimes referred to Caperton Close, was off the old Foregate (Fore Street) and was the birthplace of Alexander Kay, who, having made his fortune in insurance, gave the town money for a park and two schools.

The Carra

The Carra was a pool on the River Irvine adjacent to the Academy Playing Fields.

The Cemetery

The town's cemetery in Grassyards Road contains many fine and interesting memorials. The baronial west gatehouse facing on to Grassyards Road was built in 1875 and is of particularly interesting architecture. It bears the old burgh coat of arms.

Much of Caprington Castle is quite modern, but it goes back to a charter of 1385

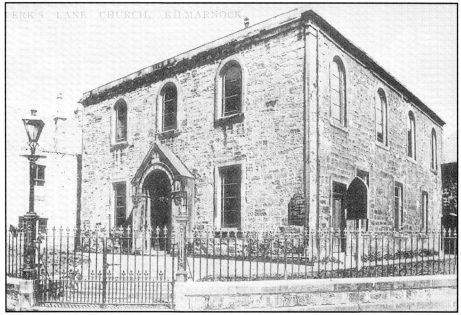

Clerk's Lane and the church here later became Kilmarnock's first cinema.

Chapman Terrace

Although the name is old, the houses in Chapman Terrace, off New Mill Road, are all new. A chapman was a street vendor.

Charles Place and Street

Charles Place and Charles Street are named after Charles Augustus, 2nd Baron Seaford and 6th Baron Howard de Walden, local landowner.

Cheapside Street

In old Scots chap was a shop; chapman a shop-man or market trader, so Cheapside Street, next to or at the side of the Cross, was probably also used by market traders. Cheapside Street has been in existence at least since the middle of the 16th century. In 1896, author George Umber said that the Cheapside Street in Kilmarnock was even more picturesque than its London namesake.

Clerk's Lane

Clerk's Lane was very narrow and zig-zagged its way to Clerk's Holm in Kay Park. It was named after William Patterson, the town clerk. Here was Clerk's Lane Church, seat of the theological revolution. The original church here was built in 1775. Under the first Minister, Rev James Robertson, the congregation outgrew the original building and it was replaced in 1807. When he died in 1811, his library of 4000 books formed the basis of the Robertsonian Library in Glasgow. In 1840 Rev James Morrison was elected minister to this church. He was at the centre of a dispute which led to the Disruption. In 1896, George Umber described the buildings in the street as: "Low decrepit thatched houses, their white washed walls grimy with weather stains."

Clans

Many of the streets in the New Farm Loch area are named after clans. They include MacIntyre, MacAdam MacInnes, MacDougall and MacBeth, as well as more than 30 others.

Clark Street

Clark Street is named after a Mr Clark of Elmbank House. The street ran alongside his land. Clark Terrace is also named after a Mr Clark of Elmbank House.

Clay Crescent

Clay Crescent is one of several groups of houses built on land once occupied by J & M Craig who were major producers of bricks and pottery.

Clay Mugs

Clay Mugs was the original name for what became Grange Street. It took its name from the location of a pottery, which used locally quarried clay.

Clerk's Holm

Clerk's Holm was an area of open space on the bank of the Kilmarnock Water. It is now part of Kay Park. It was named after the town clerk.

Climie Place

Climie Place is named after Robert Climie who became MP for Kilmarnock in 1923.

College Wynd

The Scottish Parliament - the original one - decided in 1646 that every parish in Scotland should have a school or college. The college in Kilmarnock was established near the Laigh Kirk and probably gave the name College Wynd to the street it was in. This college was burned down in the middle of the 18th century. The name, however, remained and it is one of the oldest streets in Kilmarnock. The building on the corner of College Wynd and Bank Street has a stone dated 1821 in the gable facing College Wynd.

Colquhoun Place

Colquhoun Place in New Farm Loch is named after Robert Colquhoun, a noted artist from Kilmarnock of the early 20th century.

Corrie Crescent

Corrie Crescent is a short crescent between Morven Avenue and Ardbeg Avenue, named after the village on Arran.

Cotter Drive

Cotter Drive is named in commemoration of Burn's poem, The Cotter's Saturday Night. A cotter was someone who lived in a cottage.

Cotton Street

Cotton Street was one of several streets opened in the period immediately after the improvement Act of 1804. It took its name from the number of cotton weavers in the area. It is now called Dean Street.

Craigie Road

Craigie Road is the road leading to Craigie Village and Castle. The name probably stems from the area being craggy and rocky. Craigie Castle was once described as the most magnificent castle in Ayrshire. It belonged to the Lyndsey family, passed to the Wallaces by marriage, but was abandoned by them about 400 years ago.

Croft Street before the Wheatsheaf was demolished and the facade rebuilt.

Croft Street

Croft Street was one of the very early streets of the town, dating from about the 17th century. The street was probably built on what was originally a croft field, that is the infield of a farm.

Crompton Street

Crompton Street was in Riccarton until about the 1850s when the name was changed to New Street. It is not clear who the street was originally named after.

Cross

Until the start of the 19th century the Cross was small and confined. There was a mill there until 1703, when it was moved to land close to what is now Scott Ellis playing field. In the 18th century Kilmarnock Cross was hemmed in and a row of houses went from Cheapside to the foot of Fore Street, now the Foregate. There was a narrow opening leading to Croft Street. An Improvement Act was obtained from Parliament and King Street was opened up in 1804. Portland Street was built soon after. The Cross was the heart of Kilmarnock and the venue for many key events. In 1683 covenanter, John Nisbet was executed at the Cross for resisting the king's plan to rule the church of Scotland. A stone commemorating his martyrdom was placed at the Cross. Today it is at the entrance to the Burns Shopping Centre, not far from its original position. Nisbet is buried nearby in the Laigh Kirk burial ground. The original commemoration was a collection of white stones set in the roadway. In 1843 the people of the town collected money for a statue of Sir James Shaw - Jimmie Shaw to the people of the town. He was born in

The Cross at the close of the 19th century.

Riccarton and after a brief period abroad, went into politics and became an MP in and Lord Mayor of London. Because of increased traffic the statue was moved from the Cross to its present site just off London Road, in 1929. With traffic banished from the town centre, we now have a statue of Robert Burns and John Wilson, the Kilmarnock man who first set Burns' poetry in 'guid black prent'.

Culzean Crescent

Culzean Crescent is named after the Castle and estate at Maidens. When Kilmarnock was bombed by the Luftwaffe in 1941, there were four fatalities in Culzean Crescent.

Cuthbert Place

Several street directories and maps give the name as Cuthbert or Cuthbertson Street and some as Cuthbert of Cuthbertson Place. The name may be named after a Kilmarnock Provost in 1884-1885. But he was Thomas Cuthbertson.

Dark Path

At one time The Dark Path led from Dean Castle to the road which went to Dumfries. A small portion remains near Dean Park.

David's Lane

David's Lane is another of the many street names in the town with a name of obscure origin. It might be named after David McKean who had a blacksmiths shop here.

David Orr Street

David Orr Street runs from Yorke Place towards Irvine Road, passing the modern houses of Peace Avenue, Primrose Place and Cairns Terrace.

Davie Bridge

Davie Bridge was a footbridge over the Kilmarnock Water at Kay Park, linking the park with Union Street. It was named after Bailie Robert Davie, who pushed for its construction. On one of the wrought iron gates was the word Kay and on the other the word Park, but they could only be properly read when the gates were closed.

De Walden Terrace

De Walden Terrace is a row of red sandstone houses running from Holehouse Road to the Kay Park. The name comes from Howard de Walden, local land owner. The originally gold painted street name is still visible on an end building.

Dean Castle

History is vague on the subject of the Dean Castle but it was the seat of the feudal lords of Kilmarnock. The Locarts are supposed to have built a fortification here in the 12th century. Next, perhaps, came Lord Soulis, then the Boyds. Robert Boyd fought at the battle of Largs and the Boyds later fought with Robert the Bruce in the war of independence. The castle was substantially damaged by fire in 1735 and fell into ruin, but it was restored in 1930s and given to the town in the 1970s.

Dean Lane

Dean Lane was part of the main thoroughfare from Kilmarnock to Glasgow in coaching days. From Kilmarnock going on towards Glasgow, it was an extension of High Street. The Townhead Bridge was built in 1770 close to Dean Lane. But it was narrow and steep in its earliest days.

Dean Park

Dean Park in the north of the town was opened to the public in 1907.

Dean Road

Dean Road takes its name from being the road from the town to Dean Castle and estate. In old Scots, a dean is a hollow in the land where the ground slopes on both sides.

Dean Quarry provided a great deal of the building material for Kilmarnock up to the 19th century

Douglas Street was the birthplace of poet and essayist Alexander Smith.

Dean Street

Dean Street was originally called Cotton Street. It lies on the route out of the town towards Glasgow. A block of council-built flats on the corner of Witch Road and Dean Street has the date 1955 on the balconies.

Dean Terrace

Dean Terrace is one of several streets opened up or expanded between 1851 and 1879. It forms part of the main thoroughfare and is between Dean Street and Beansburn.

Dean View Place

Dean View Place is a block of tenement flats and is part of Beansburn on the main thoroughfare going out of Kilmarnock towards Glasgow. The name is inscribed at one end of the block. On the other end there is Dean View Villa.

Dick Road

Dick Road was named after James Dick who did a great deal to promote the idea of a library, museum and art hall. That idea became the Dick Institute.

Douglas Street

Originally, Douglas Street was known as Shuttle Street. This street links Titchfield Street and the Howard Park and was the birthplace of poet and writer, Alexander Smith (1829-1867). A stone marks the site of the cottage where he was born. Close to the Douglas Street bridge there was a spring which, until the advent of piped water, was considered to have the best drinking water in the town. Once again the origin of the newer name is uncertain. The name may relate to James Douglas a local artist of some note.

Drumclog Place

Drumclog Place is named after the village of Drumclog in Lanarkshire. It was the scene of a clash in 1679 which resulted in an important victory for the Covenanters.

Duke Street

Duke Street was opened in 1859. Called Victoria Street during the construction, it linked the Cross and London Road. It consisted of fine architecture, but was demolished in the 1970s to make way for a shopping centre.

Dundonald Road

Dundonald Road was one of many streets opened up or expanded between 1811 and 1851 when the town's population more than doubled. The route that existed before being widened was known as the Bullet Road. The first house in Dundonald Road was Wards House, built in 1828. The straight wide road we know today dated from the middle of the 18th century. At the corner of Dundonald Road and Portland Road is the Holy Trinity Church, a building of fine architecture in a traditional English style. This church has a garden of remembrance containing an old mile stone and, less obviously, the remnants of an old well. This church, along with its neighbour, is in a part of Dundonald Road once known as Winton Place. The town's Grammar School was on the corner of Dundonald Road and St Marnock Street. The site is now occupied by the Sheriff Court House.

Dunlop Street

This street was named after James Dunlop who owned Langlands House.

Dundonald Road just before the start of the age of the car.

Dunollie Gardens

Dunollie Gardens in the Southcraig development takes its name from Dunollie Castle, near Oban.

Dunure

Dunure Drive off London Road and Dunure Place in Southcraig take their names from Dunure south of Ayr. Dunure is best remembered for the roasting of Allan Stewart, Commendator of Crossraguel Abbey, by Gilbert Kennedy.

East George Street

East George Street was known as Paddy's Brae before being reconstructed into a street which was fit enough to be named after the king (George III).

East Netherton Street

East Netherton Street was a thoroughfare in 1770. It ran from the Netherton to the whinstone quarry, which was in front of what is now St. Andrew's Church. In 1875 East Netherton Street was described as a very old street, mostly of thatched cottages. At one time it was mostly occupied by weavers.

East Shaw Street

In 1875 Archibald Adamson said of East Shaw Street: (It) has not an elegant appearance. The houses are, with few exceptions, of one storey and covered with thatch. Here, however, was Shawbank, said to be a handsome villa. East Shaw Street was formerly Glen Street and was renamed in honour of Sir James Shaw, the Riccarton man who became MP and Lord Mayor of London.

Elderslie Crescent

Elderslie Crescent is named after Elderslie in Renfrewshire, which claims to be the birthplace of Sir William Wallace, the great hero of the war of independence. Recent controversy has surrounded this claim and a counter claim says that Wallace was born closer to home, at Ellerslie near Kilmarnock. Elderslie Crescent consists of council houses and one block bears the date 1927.

Ellis Street

Ellis Street takes its name from one of the family names associated with the Howard de Walden family. The name also appears in Scott-Ellis.

Ellisland Drive

Ellisland was the farm, six miles from Dumfries, taken by Robert Burns in 1788.

Elmbank

Elmbank Drive takes its name from Elmbank House which was demolished to make way for the Dick Institute. Originally Elmbank was called Lewisville but the name was changed after the building was greatly extended. Elmbank was acquired by the town and used as a library, but was later demolished to clear the site for the construction of the Dick Institute. Elmbank Avenue also takes its name from Elmbank House.

Esson Place

Esson is an old Scots family name. It is not a common name and it is no longer known just who this street is named after.

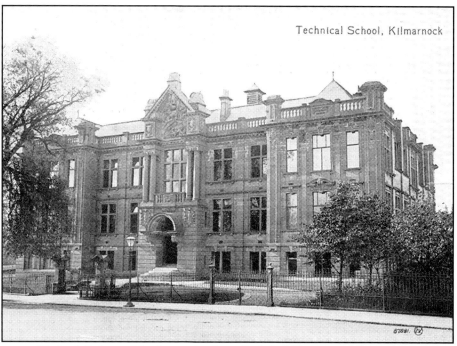

Technical School, Kilmarnock

Elmbank Drive and the former Academy Tech. building, now sadly neglected.

Fairyhill

The Fairy Hill was a feature on Holmes Farm. There was also the Fairyholm. Into the early years of the 20th Century there was a row of whitewashed cottages near the original hill. Today the road alongside the Kilmarnock Water leading to the hill is Fairyhill Road. Most of the houses in Fairyhill Road are early 20th century. Some have been prone to flooding, but in the late 1990s a flood wall was built on the banks of the river. No connection with fairy folklore has been found.

Fairlie Avenue

Fairlie Avenue is named after Fairlie House, or Fairlie Five Lums, as the locals called it. The house is near Gatehead.

Firs Brae

The sharply rising road that is now Park Street was once known as The Firs Brae because of a line of fir trees there. The trees were the boundary of the estate of Langlands. When the gas works were built, it became the Gas Brae.

Fleshmarket Bridge

The Fleshmarket Bridge over the Kilmarnock Water was built in 1770 and linked Waterloo Street and Market Place, later Market Lane. There were shops on this bridge and at one time, as the name implies, it was the market place for meat. Before the bridge was built the market was held on the Sandbed Bridge. In 1852 the bridge was destroyed by a severe flood, but the old datestone was incorporated into the new bridge and a stone marking the flood was also built into it. The bridge was removed in the 1970s to make way for the Burns Shopping Centre.

Fore Street

Fore Street was one of the very early streets of the town, dating from at least 1550. It takes its name from at one time being the main street of the town. It was commonly called the Fore Gait, and today is the Foregate. In the middle of the 18th century it was one of the preferred streets for the homes of the merchants, but houses were small and badly ventilated. In June of 1863 workmen taking down an old inn at the foot of Fore Street

Fore Street was once the main street in Kilmarnock.

found a remarkable collection of old coins, which were probably hidden in Covenanting times. Archibald Adamson painted a grim picture of the street in Rambles Round Kilmarnock (1875). He said the Foregate ' is a narrow, confined thoroughfare, lined on both sides with low roofed, old fashioned houses. Their ground floors are mostly occupied with brokers' shops, at the doors of which furniture, old boots, and clothing of every description are exposed for sale.' And added: 'Unwashed children gambol in the gutter, and poverty stricken men and women jostle each other as they pass up an down.' In 1896 writer, George Umber agreed it was narrow and tortuous but added that it had a 'delightful huddlement of angles and gables, and chimney stacks and outside stairs.' In 1898 historian, artist and architect, Thomas Smellie said: 'The Foregate is rich in interesting 'bits' but a good fire would probably be no great calamity.'

Foregate

The original name for Fore Street was Fore Gait, meaning the main street or main entrance into the town. The name was later Anglicised and was readopted when the present Foregate was opened in the 1970s. Look at the flagstones at the entrance to the shops. Each is crafted to suit the trader.

Foregate Square

Foregate Square is the open space between the Foregate and the Burns Shopping Centre. Of 1970s vintage, it contains some items of modern art including an obscure dustbin like feature which commemorates town twinning agreements with towns in France, Germany, Belgium and Abkhazia. There is also a stone laid flush to the ground, also connected with town twinning. The Gateway building has ornate sculpted features. Here also is the main entrance to the bus station, revamped several times since it was opened in the 1970s.

Forge Street

Forge Street was not always a straight road as it is today. In the 1930s it took a dog leg turn. This street takes its name from its proximity to the former Portland Forge.

Foundry Street

In the 1840s Foundry Street was little more than a path that ran from the end of Park Street to a collection of engineering works and foundries. Part of the path became a part of North Hamilton Street and part became Forge Street.

Fowlds Street

When built what became Fowlds Street ran through land owned by Alexander Fowlds, who operated a nursery and seed business. Of note today is the Baptist Church, and the Sovereign Grace Church, both small, plain but very functional.

Fullarton Street

Fullarton Street is another link to the Duke of Portland, whose family seat was at Welbeck Abbey in Nottinghamshire. At the start of the 19th century, the Marquis of Titchfield, later the Duke of Portland, bought the ancient estate of Fullarton in Troon. Between 1808 and 1812 he built the Kilmarnock and Troon Railway. In 1897 a piece of waste ground here was cleared by enthusiastic volunteers to create Springhill Bowling Club.

Fulton's Lane

It is no longer certain which Fulton is commemorated in Fulton's Lane, which was originally Rackhead. It may be John Fulton, the Fenwick shoemaker who built an orrery which is still on display in the Transport Museum in Glasgow. An orrery is a mechanical model of the solar system which shows the relative motions of the planets and their moons. Fulton's Lane consisted of mean looking houses, but in one of them the town's first ever laundry was established. Some council houses were built here in the 1920s.

Gallion Brae

The Gallion Brae lay just off Titchfield Street and East Netherton Street, close to the present houses of St Andrew Terrace. The roadway here was levelled off by the unemployed in 1816. The spoil was used to fill in the Netherton Quarry, which was in front of the church in St Andrew Street. In 1875 the only houses here formed a row of old thatched cottages that sat above the level of the road.

Gallows-knowe

The Gallows-knowe was the hill where the gibbet was erected in the days of feudalism for hanging thieves and other criminals. The first dissenting church was built here in 1772.

Garden Street

Garden Street was the lane previously known as the Back o' the Yards. Perhaps gardens became more socially acceptable than yards. At one time it extended from its junction with West George Street, went under the railway and joined Portland Street and Wellington Street where they meet.

Gargieston

Gargieston, on the road from Kilmarnock to Gatehead, was once the site of extensive tileworks, which made goods for drainage and farming. The name lives on in the local primary school.

Gas Brae

What is now Park Street became known as the Gas Brae when the gas works were built there early in the 19th century. It had previously been Firs Brae. Hugh Muir Nelson was born here. He became the Prime Minister of Queensland and was later the Lieutenant Governor of the colony.

Gibson Street

Gibson Street was probably named after John Gibson, a Kilmarnock writer.

Glebe Road early in the 20th century.

Gillsburn

Gillsburn appears on maps of the late 18th century on the Glasgow Road, but it is yet another old name of obscure origin. Townholm had a Gillsburn Place, a street mostly of red sandstone tenements, and today the town still has Gillsburn Gardens.

Gilmour Street

Gilmour Street was one of several streets opened up or expanded between 1851 and 1879. It may be named after the builder responsible for the work there. In the 1970s the buildings in Gilmour Street were demolished and modern council houses built in their place, including the town's 10,000th council home.

Glasgow Road

Glasgow Road is the road extending from Dean Street out of town in the direction of Glasgow.

Glebe

The glebe usually refers to land around a manse and in Kilmarnock there is a Glebe Avenue and a Glebe Road. They are both residential streets.

Glen Street

Glen Street, named after the profusion of daffodils - or glens - was renamed Shaw Street in honour of Sir James Shaw, the Riccarton man who became Lord Mayor of London.

Glencairn Square

Glencairn Square was opened up in 1765 and until the 20th century was generally known as the Holm Square. In April 1800, fire swept through the square and surrounding streets, destroying many houses and the Holm School. In 1875 Archibald Adamson said of Glencairn Square: "The Square is spacious, but the buildings in it, with two or three exceptions, are thatched, low roofed, dingy dwellings". When the Co-op built premises at the top of Low Glencairn Street, a clock was put on the wall facing the square. Locals confused visitors by telling them that 'The square clock is round'.

Glencairn Street

Glencairn Street was the original name for High and Low Glencairn Street.

Glenfield Place

Glenfield Place and Glenfield Gardens are built on land that was occupied by Glenfield and Kennedy, once one of the world's biggest producers of hydraulic and water equipment.

Goosegog Field

Up until the 1960s, a field off Nursery Avenue was known as Goosegog Field. It was a popular play area for children until it was built on. The houses there form Mitchell Court.

Gooselet Park

An area of ground bounded by Strawberrybank Road and South Dean Road appears on late 18th century maps marked as Gooselet Park.

Grange

Formerly, the Grange was a farm close to town. It is now the name of a housing estate.

Grange Street

Originally Grange Street was called the Clay Mugs and was once the home of Greenshields Brewery. Thomas Greenshields, who once ran the brewery there was a close friend of Robert Burns. The street was also the home of James and William Tannock, brothers who made names for themselves as artists.

Grange Terrace

Grange Terrace is one of several streets opened up or expanded between 1851 and 1879. It was home to several prominent business people.

Grassyards Road

Grassyards is a farm near the Fenwick to Galston Road. The Grassyards Road leads out of town towards Grassyards Farm. Until the 1960s it was a popular country walk and today it is an important feeder road serving the New Farm Loch area. Here is the main entrance to Kilmarnock cemetery.

Great Hamilton Street

Land on which Great Hamilton Street was built was owned by the Hamilton family. The street later became North and South Hamilton Street.

Green Brae

Before Kay Park was opened the hill near the Townhead Bridge was planted as gardens and with trees. The entrance was known as the Green Brae, described as "a pleasant little grassy walk".

Green Bridge

Originally built in 1759, the Green Bridge replaced an earlier ford and created a new exit from the town centre towards Hurlford and the towns of the Irvine Valley. The old bridge was replaced in the 1970s.

This rather gothic building is the gatehouse to the cemetry in Grasslands Road.

Green Street and Kilmarnock's first Fire Brigade Station.

Green Street

The Town Green, once fairly extensive, was off what's now London Road. Green Street led to the town green.

Greenfoot

Greenfoot was the street between the Cross and the foot of the town Green. After the battle of Waterloo in 1815, the street was renamed Waterloo Street. Here was the pub that became the Tam O' Shanter. In a corner of the outside wall was a heart with the initials of presumably the first occupants of the building and the date 1761.

Greenhead

As the name implies Greenhead was at the head of the town's green and was first commercially developed in 1743 when permission was granted to build a 'woollen manufactory' there.

Greenholm Street

A descriptive name for what was once a flat grassy area near the river close to what is now the Riccarton Bridge. There was a quarry near here known as the holm quarry. The area became home to Barclay's engineering works and later the burgh power and tram depot.

Guard Lane

When the town jail was in the Townhouse in King Street, the land leading to it was called Guard Lane. A small portion of this street still exists between the BHS store and the Halifax Building Society.

Hamilton Place

Hamilton Place was named after the Hamilton family who owned the land on which the street was built.

Harperland Drive

Harperland Drive is named after Harperland Farm about half way between Kilmarnock and Dundonald.

Harriet Street

Harriet Street was one of the first streets in the Townholm area of Kilmarnock. When the area was used mostly for engineering works in the middle of the 19th century, the only roads or streets with names were Townholm and Harriet Street.

Hatter's Laun

Hatter's Laun or Land was part of Tankardha' Brae for many years. The area was named after Robert Barnes, a hatter who set up business here in 1730. Hat making continued on the site until about the 1840s.

Hawket Park

Hawket Park was the name of a private house, close to what is now Hill Street. Early maps show a few buildings here. The Hawket Park was between Kilmaurs Road, Wellington Street and what was later named Witch Road.

Henrietta Street

Henrietta Street is named after Henrietta Scott who was a local landowner when she married the Marquis of Titchfield, son of the Duke of Portland.

High Bonnyton Road

High Bonnyton Road ran from Hill Street, almost to where Balmoral Road is now. It existed until the expansion of Johnnie Walkers whisky plant in Hill Street.

This is High Street once one of the principal streets of the town.

High Church

High Church Lane led to the High Church. When the parish church (Laigh Kirk) became overcrowded, a new church was required and the one that was built became the High Church, now the oldest church building in the town. It was built in 1731. Several interesting graves can be found in the kirkyard including memorials to Thomas Kennedy, inventor of the water meter; John Wilson, printer of Burns poems; the Tannock brothers, artists; and Thomas Morton, engineer and astronomer.

High Glencairn Street

High Glencairn Street was opened up in 1765 by the Earl of Glencairn as part of the main route between Kilmarnock and Riccarton.

High Street

High Street was one of the very early streets of the town, dating from at least the 17th century. The Meal Market was here, built in 1705 and rebuilt in 1840. In the middle of the 18th century it was one of the preferred streets for the homes of the merchants, but houses were small and badly ventilated. In 1865 the street was described as a narrow thoroughfare in three parts. The other parts were Soulis Street and Fore Street.

Hill Street

Hill Street has been known since the 1950s as the home of Johnnie Walker whisky. Hill Street also contains St Joseph's Church and Nazareth House, both buildings of fine architectural merit. The church opened in 1847 and Nazareth House in 1890, when it was a home for orphans and old people. The hill in the name was known as Sheilin Hill.

Hillhead

A map of the town as it was in 1783, but drawn some years later, shows Hillhead as a farm to the north and west of the town and well away from any built up developments. Today the name is used for a general area of the town.

Hills

A group of streets in Bellfield is named after Scottish hills and mountains. They include Sidlaw, Kinnoul, Cuillin, Leadhills, Cairngorm, Ochil and Grampian.

Hole in the Wa'

Most towns appear have had a 'hole in the wall'. Kilmarnock's was situated behind Cheapside between the Sandbed Bridge and Morris Place. The name was later adopted by a tavern in the vicinity and a well there was known by the same name.

Holehouse Road

Holehouse was a farm near the town. The original name for this street was Hollis Road. The rector of Kilmarnock Academy had for many years a tied house at the corner of London Road and Holehouse Road. The Technical College was built in Holehouse Road in the 1960s. Some of the town's first council houses were built here in the early 1920s.

Holm Square

Holm Square was the former name of Glencairn Square. The land here was developed by the Earl of Glencairn in 1765. Prior to this time it has been a market square. It was also the place of the Holm Parliament, where disenfranchised men would meet to discuss politics and plan for a better world.

Holmes Road

A holm is flat low lying ground on the inside of the curve of a river plain and this description gave its name to Holmes Farm and a number of streets in the area, such as the Holm Square and Holmquarry Road.

Holmhead

Holmhead was the top part of Titchfield Street near the junction with King Street.

Holmquarry Road

There was a quarry on the Kilmarnock side of the River Irvine which was always the holm quarry because it was in the holm of the river. From this, fine sandstone was quarried for many years. The site of the quarry continued to appear on maps of the 1850s, though by then it is described as an old quarry. Other early maps show this area as Sandy Holm. After the quarry closed the area belonged to a builder, then to Kilmarnock Cricket Club, who were forced to sell it to the town in 1902 for the power station and tram depot.

Holmes Road

Holmes Road was the road leading to Holmes Farm. The local golf and cricket clubs played here before establishing their own grounds. Holmes Farm became the Dairy School for Scotland, the forerunner of today's Scottish Agricultural School. When the Agricultural School moved to Auchencruive, the buildings at Holmes became a maternity hospital and today it is the Strathlee Centre.

Hood Street

Hood Street was named after James Hood, a Provost of Kilmarnock. In the 1920s houses to a unique architectural design were built here by Johnnie Walker for their employees. After years of neglect by the local authority they were controversially demolished towards the end of the 20th century.

Whisky giants Johnnie Walker had these houses in Hood Street built for their workers.

Howard Park has a memorial to those who died in our twin town of Sukhum during the war between Abkhazia and Georgia.

Howard Park

Parts of the area now known as Howard Park have been known as Wards Park and Barbadoes Green and was originally part of the grounds of Kilmarnock House. The park in its present form was given to the town by Lord Howard de Walden and opened as a public park in 1894. It contains a mass grave to the 250 victims of the 1832 cholera outbreak, a memorial to local doctor, Alexander Marshall and a memorial dedicated to citizens of Sukhum who were killed in the civil war of 1992-93 following the collapse of the Soviet empire. Sukhum, originally Sukhumi in Abkhazia is twinned with Kilmarnock. When the town dropped the final 'I' the Howard Park monument was altered to keep it correct. In the park you can still trace the original course of the Kilmarnock Water by following a high banking. The route along it is known as the Lady's Walk. One of the roads leading to the park is Howard Park Drive.

Howard Street

Howard Street is named after Lord Howard de Walden.

Hurlford Road

Hurlford Road is now a main artery to the Bellfield Interchange. In 1960, 14 years before the by pass and the Bellfield Interchange were built, Hurlford Road won a Civic Trust award for its good design of keeping traffic and pedestrians apart. There is a plaque marking the award in Hurlford Road.

Inchgotrick Road

Inchgotrick was a farm to the south of Kilmarnock. It was the birthplace of George Cunningham, who wrote poetry and newspaper articles under the name of Pate McPhun.

India Street

India Street was probably named in commemoration of the trading links with India built up by the Buchanan family of Bellfield House.

Ingram Place

Ingram Place is named after James Ingram, a local architect responsible for the Palace Theatre, the Dick Institute and other prominent buildings in the area.

Inkerman Place

Inkerman Place is just off Fullarton Street, facing on to the Bonnyton Road. It is named after the battle at Inkerman Ridge in 1854, during the Crimean war.

Islands

A group of streets in Onthank is named after Scottish Islands including Lewis, Iona, Benbecula, Harris and Ailsa.

Irvine Bank

Irvine Bank is at the road along the bank of the River Irvine.

Irvine Road

Irvine Road is one of many streets opened up or expanded between 1811 and 1851 when the town's population more than doubled. It replaced what became Old Irvine Road.

James Little Street

Although at right angles to Bentinck Street, James Little Street was part of Bentinck Street until 1872 when Bentinck Street was extended to East Shaw Street. The part which linked Bentinck Street to High Glencairn Street was then named James Little Street after a mill owner and magistrate.

Jeffrey Street

When Riccarton was an independent parish and had its own Academy, the school playing fields were at what is now Jeffrey Street.

John Dickie Street

John Dickie was a seed merchant and at one time was Provost of Kilmarnock. The street that now bears his name was built in 1876 on what was at one time part of the Laigh Kirk graveyard. During excavations for the construction of the street many skeletons were exhumed. The old Kilmarnock Town Chambers are here and still bear the name Wallace Chambers after William Wallace - the local whisky baron. Johnnie Walker eventually took over Wallace's business and ultimately had extensive property in John Dickie Street and the adjacent Strand. The street has a statue of Johnnie Walker looking across the road to buildings in the Strand that were built for his company's whisky empire.

John Finnie Street

John Finnie Street was one of several streets opened up or expanded from the middle of the 19th century. John Finnie, coal owner, paid a substantial part of the costs of the development of the street. Today it is held as an outstanding example of planned Victorian architecture and many of the fine buildings there have dates on them. One outstanding feature is that all the buildings, with one exception, are predominately of red stone. One of the fine buildings that has been lost was originally built as an opera house. It also served as a church and a night club - though not at the same time. It was destroyed by fire and today the facade hides an undeveloped gap site.

John Finnie Street in the early years of the 20th century.

Judas Hill

Judas Hill is close to where the Craufurdland Water joins the Fenwick Water to form the Kilmarnock Water. It is said by some to have been the Justine Hill on which criminals, some of them petty thieves, were executed. One tradition says that men killed in battle were buried there, but that is unlikely.

Judgement Hill

The Judgement Hill or Justice Mound were names used in the 19th century for the hill - probably artificial - on which the Riccarton Church was built.

Kadikoi Place

Kadikoi Place is that part of Bonnyton which was being developed shortly after the time of the Crimean war and names such as Kadikoi, Inkerman and probably Ava all relate to that conflict.

Kay Park

Kay Park was developed out of land at Clerk's Holm and other areas. The park was opened in 1879 with money given to the town by Alexander Kay, a Kilmarnock man who made his fortune in Glasgow from insurance. The park contains the now disused monument to Robert Burns. Although boarded up and fenced off now, it originally contained a museum. Fine views of the Ayrshire countryside were obtained from the top of the monument. Near the monument is a disused fountain, given to the town by James Craig in commemoration of the coronation of Edward VII. A short walk away there is the monument to the reformers who campaigned for a universal franchise. A liberty statue on top of the column was blown off in a storm in 1936 and has never been replaced. At one time the park contained a fine cast iron fountain made at Coalbrookdale but it was scrapped

Kay Park and the Burns Monument.

during World War II. An ornate bandstand was also removed. If you enter the park from the London Road entrance you will see two stone pillars in the fence just beyond the railway viaduct. They are all that is left of a footbridge over the Kilmarnock Water. This bridge had a decorative wrought iron gate. On one half was the word 'Kay' and on the other was 'Park' so the name could be read when the gates were closed. The bridge was removed in the 1970s. Alexander Kay also left the town money for schools in Wellington Street and Bentinck Street.

Kay Park Crescent

Kay Park Crescent is a row of houses on the edge of Kay Park.

Kay Park Lane

Kay Park Lane appears to be an unofficial name for the lane leading from London Road, alongside Henderson Church, the bowling club, tennis courts and into the Kay Park.

Kay Park Terrace

Kay Park Terrace is a row of houses on the edge of the Kay Park. The post box here has the scarce EviiiR insignia.

Kelk Place

Kelk Place, pronounced Kelp, was a row of miners' cottages on the road between Kilmarnock and Crosshouse. They were just opposite what is now the Ellerslie Inn.

Kennedy Street

Kennedy Street was named after Thomas Kennedy, a local gunsmith and engineer who invented a much improved water meter and set up Glenfield and Kennedy which became the biggest hydraulic engineering concern in the British Empire.

Kilgour Terrace

Kilgour Terrace is part of Bonnyton Road on the town side of Munro Avenue. The houses were named after the wife of the builder, a D Ramsay of Saint Andrew Street. On the opposite side of Munro Avenue the houses are known as Ava Terrace. The names are etched into the stonework.

Kilmarnock House Avenue

This avenue was marked on a map of 1819 and was close to Kilmarnock House in what later became Saint Marnock Street.

Kilmarnock Water

The Kilmarnock Water is one of two rivers flowing through the town. The Kilmarnock Water is formed near Dean Castle where the Fenwick Water and the Craufurdland Water meet. It flows through the town to join the River Irvine at Riccarton. In former days it was a source of water, building sand and stones and was used to take away sewage.

Kilmaurs Road

The road leaving Kilmarnock in the direction of Kilmaurs was originally an extension of Witch Road and was sometimes referred to as Kilmaurs Brae. Today Kilmaurs Road is off the Western Road. It was developed for council housing in the 1930s.

King Street

King Street was opened up in 1804 as the principal thoroughfare of the town and was named after King George III. The date 1805 appears on the gable of one of the buildings near the cross. Before King Street was opened there were several narrow twisting streets and lanes in the congested area around the Cross - Streets and neuks, as Burns put it. The opening of King Street transformed the appearance of Kilmarnock. The street was wide, long and straight - everything all the other streets of the town were not. It contained the Town House and local jail, now demolished. Other fine buildings in this street included King Street Church, also now demolished and various banks, also demolished. It was in King Street that Johnnie Walker opened his first grocery and spirit shop in 1821 on a site very close to a narrow and unnamed passage to the Sandbed. Many of King Street's fine buildings were demolished to make way for 1970's shoe box architecture which obscures a fine view of the former Royal Bank building at the Cross. One building that did survive is now used by the Halifax Building Society. When proposals to demolish most of one side of the street were announced in the early 1970s, the owners of that building - at the time Graftons - objected on the grounds that it was a new building. They won their case. Some interesting buildings remain. A red sandstone building at the corner of Water Lane has musical instruments carved in the stonework. Street art in King Street includes acrobatic bin men on some of the waste paper bins and swimmers' heads which mark where the Kilmarnock Water flows below the street.

This is King Street at the end of the 19th century.

The Swimmer, a feature of today's King Street.

Kingswell Avenue

Kingswell Avenue was named after King's Well close to the Eaglesham turn off on what is now the A77. Here one of the Scottish kings is supposed to have rested and refreshed his men and horses. It was the location of a popular inn in coaching days.

Kirkhaugh

The land between the Laigh Kirk and the river bank was named Kirkhaugh before being levelled in 1710 and built on to form Bank Street.

Kirklandside

Kirklandside, close to the Bellfield roundabout, was opened as a fever hospital in 1909.

Kirkstyle

Kirkstyle was a farm in Riccarton parish before the town grew to absorb its lands. There was a Kirkstyle coal pit in this area and after it closed the land was used by Glacier Metal. The school in the area is still the Kirkstyle School.

Kirktonholm

Kirktonholm Street was one of several streets which was greatly redeveloped in the 1870s. A century later the area was demolished and a new Kirktonholm Street and a Kirktonholm Place were built.

Knockinlaw

Coal was worked in the area of Knockinlaw or Knockinglaw from at least the 1780s and probably much earlier.

Knockinlaw Mount

Earthworks marked as Knockinlaw Mount were noted on old maps. Today the area is bounded by Knockinlaw Road, Burnfoot Place and, Onthank Drive. The name is a curious mixture of three languages: knock is Scots Gaidhlig; law is old Scots and mount is English. Together the term Knockinlaw Mount translates as the hill hill hill.

Knockmarloch Drive

Knockmarloch Drive in Shortlees is named after the farm of Knockmarloch. The farm land is now used for housing. Knockmarloch was the birthplace of John Burtt. As a teenager he was press-ganged and spent five years at sea. He was a campaigner for the extension of the franchise and spent his later years in the USA as a minister.

Ladeside Street

A lade once ran from the Kilmarnock Water to the old mill at the Cross. The mill was removed in 1703, but the names involved continued. Ladeside Street was originally beside that lade close to the railway viaduct.

Lady's Walk

The walk is in what is now Howard Park and the Lady was the wife of William Boyd, the lord of Kilmarnock. He chose to fight on the wrong side during the rebellion of 1745 and his wife is said to have frequently walked through the parkland as she waited for news of her husband's trial in London. He was found guilty of treason and executed. The river at one time flowed at the base of it.

The Lady's Walk, in Howard Park, named after Lady Kilmarnock.

The Laigh Kirk graveyard has several interesting grave stones, like this one to Covenanter John Nisbet.

Laigh Kirk

It is said that the Laigh Kirk is saturated in history. There has been a church on or near this site since the town was a mere hamlet. The earliest part of the present building is the base of the tower and it is dated 1410. Incidents over patronage in this church inspired fine works from Burns. In 1801 disaster overwhelmed the congregation when they thought the building was falling down and in the mad stampede to get out 29 people died. After that the old building was demolished and the present one built with numerous exits including one directly from the pulpit to Bank Street. The church graveyard used to go all the way down to the river and included parts of what is now John Dickie Street. The present graveyard includes several memorials to contemporaries of Burns and to Covenanters as well as various other people of note. Until the middle of the 18th century the Laigh Kirk was known simply as the church. It

adopted the Laigh title to distinguish it from the new or High Church. Attempts to Anglicise the name have never been successful but today we have Low Church Lane and the inscription on the lamp posts at the main entrance read 'Low Church'.

Landsborough Drive

Landsborough Drive is named after the Rev Dr David Landsborough who spent his life in Kilmarnock as the minister of Henderson Church. He was also a naturalist of note and a local historian.

Langlands

The estate of Langlands existed outside the built up area of Kilmarnock but was absorbed as the town grew. It was owned by the Dalrymple family who sold it to the Dunlops of Annanhill in the 1830s. They started feuing the land for development. Today there is Langlands Brae, Langlands Street and West Langlands Street.

Lang Stane Dyke

Parts of this dry stane dyke remained until the start of the 19th century. It was a perimeter wall around much of the lands of the Dean Castle, built with stones taken from the fields and the river. It extended at least from the foot of Willie Mair's Brae to Assloss.

Lauder Bridge

The Lauder Bridge over the Kilmarnock Water is close to the Dean Ford on Dean Street. The present bridge is not the original one. The first Lauder Bridge collapsed on the day it was opened. Its name comes from David Lauder, who did so much to get a footbridge built. He owned a shop in King Street known as Lauder's Emporium.

Lawson Street

Lawson Street is named after John Lawson who owned the Loanhead wool mill which was situated in this area.

Lillymount Place

Lillymount Place is one of the red sandstone tenement terraces making up Old Mill Road. The name is still visible, but only just, on the corner of Dick Road and Old Mill Road, opposite Alexandra Place.

Lindsay Street

Lindsay Street is probably named after Rev William Lindsay, the first of the 'new licht' ministers in Kilmarnock, whose riotous induction was the inspiration for Burns poem, 'The Ordination'.

Loan, The

In Contributions to Local History (1878) Rev David Landsborough said that old folk still referred to East and West Shaw Streets as The Loan. A loan was an opening between cornfields, used for driving the cattle. From this we also have Loanhead Street and Loanfoot Avenue.

This is Lawson Street and the building is Fleming's lace mill.

London Road in the days when trees did not constitute a traffic hazard.

Loanfoot Avenue

Loanfoot Avenue was the road leading to Loanfoot House which later became Annanhill House.

Loanhead Street

Andrew Carnegie came to Kilmarnock to lay the foundation stone of the Loanhead School which is in Loanhead Street. The street also has a small area of open park which contains the remains of a fountain commemorating the Kilmarnock Co-op. The Loanhead Garden here was opened in 1937.

London Road

London Road runs from near the town centre almost to Crookedholm. The London Road Bridge over the Kilmarnock Water has the date 1827 on a stone on each side of the river. Just across the Kilmarnock Water, on the right side going out of town, there is a building used for sports. I was once told that this was originally constructed as a World War II air raid shelter, but I have been unable to confirm this. In 1837 the unemployed were put to work to cut out the hill between Braehead House and Rosebank, the home of Tam Samson. Tam Samson was a friend and patron of Robert Burns and today a neglected plaque marks the site of the house. Tam Samson is buried in the grounds of the Laigh Kirk. At the corner of London Road and Holehouse Road there is a rose garden and at one corner of this, on London Road, there is an old milestone. James Hamilton High School was near the far end of the street and the building is now the headquarters of East Ayrshire Council. Among the important buildings in London Road today is the Palace Theatre and Grand Hall.

Longpark

Longpark began to be developed for council houses in the 1930s.

Low Church Lane

The Laigh Kirk was the focus around which Kilmarnock grew. Until 1731 it was the only church in Kilmarnock and did not have a name. In 1731 when the growing population required another church, the new one was called the High Kirk and the old the Laigh Kirk. Attempts over the years to Anglicise the name have always failed and this name is a reminder of those attempts.

Low Glencairn Street

Low Glencairn Street is part of the thoroughfare from Kilmarnock, through the Netherton and on to Riccarton. It was opened up in 1765 by the Earl of Glencairn.

Low Green

The Town Green was split into the Low Green and High Green by what is now London Road. In 1807 the Academy was built there and today the site is occupied by the Grand Hall.

Mack's Corner

Mack's Corner was part of the junction of King Street, Titchfield Street and Fowlds Street, It was near here in 1900 that an ancient urn was found containing what appeared to be three neolithic arrowheads.

Manse Street

The Manse of the Laigh Kirk originally stood on open space, but land around it was gradually built on. Even though the manse was relocated, the name persists.

MANSE STREET, KILMARNOCK.

Manse Street about 100 years ago.

McKinlay Place and the house with a plaque marking the 3,000th council house.

Market Lane

Market Lane was originally known as Water Lane. This was the lane that led to the flesh market. After King Street was opened, the remains of Market Lane became just one of the minor lanes off the new street. Here was Begbie's Inn, mentioned by Burns. After some major rebuilding Begbie's building became the Angel inn and later still the Angel Hotel. In later days it was the Albion Bar. Before the building was demolished in the 1970s it was part of Woolworths.

Maxholm Road

Maxholm was a farm close to the meeting of the Kilmarnock Water and the River Irvine where the Maxholm burn ran into the Irvine. today we have Maxholm Road.

McKinlay Place

McKinlay Place and McKinlay Terrace are named after Rev James McKinlay, minister of the Laigh Kirk and an associate of Burns. A house here used to have a plaque noting that it was the 3000th house built by Kilmarnock Corporation. The house is still there but the plaque is not.

MacLelland Drive

MacLelland Drive is named after Archibald MacLelland who was once the Provost of Kilmarnock. There are fine villas here, and note that many still have their original railings and a few are rather ornate. They were not removed during the war because the street was still used to drive cattle from the market to the slaughter house.

Meiklewood

Meiklewood Farm lies to the north of the town. When the A77 eastern by-pass was built in 1974, Meiklewood gave its name to the intersection there.

Melville Street

Melville Street was developed for council housing in the 1930s.

Menford Lane

The route of Menford Lane was originally Menfuird or Menfurd. The lands were extensive and were acquired by the Lord Boyd in 1612. The name is said to come from the Wallaces of Menfurd who owned land here.

Mill Court

Forming part of Old Mill Road, the special sheltered housing complex of Mill Court was opened in 1987 to give independence and security to tenants in a town centre location.

Mill Lane

This was a connecting lane between Mill Road and New Mill Road. Originally it was called Between the Dykes.

Mill Road

Mill Road. is now Old Mill Road, to distinguish it from New Mill Road. The old mill was at the Cross, the new mill near the river at what is now Scott Ellis.

Mill Street

Mill Street led to the Netherton Mill rather than the town mill.

Milldykes

Milldykes, sometimes referred to as Mill Dykes, was part of the route from London Road to Struthers Steps, but including other land as well such as where Richardland Road was built.

Miller's Dam

The Miller's Dam on the River Irvine near Crookedholm was in situ for many years after its use was discontinued. It was demolished in 1985.

Mitchell Court

Mitchell Court was built on the Goosegog Field just off Nursery Avenue. It is not clear who is commemorated in the name.

Montgomery Street

Montgomery Street dates from the early part of the 20th century. It is off Balmoral Road and Hill Street and takes its name from Alexander Montgomery who was a local poet. Near here is Montgomery Place. Both are off Hill Street.

Morris Lane

Morris Lane is off Boyd Street, which was previously known as Morris Street. It leads to Fulton's Lane. William Morris was a local bailie.

Morris Place

Morris Place was an area behind Cheapside a little downstream from the Sandbed Bridge and facing on to King Street. It was named after James Morris, a carrier who spent 70 years travelling between Kilmarnock and Glasgow.

Morris Street

What became Boyd Street was originally Mountgean, where gean or wild cherry trees grew, then New Raw, presumably after houses were built, then Morris Street, which was named after William Morris, a local bailie.

Morton Place

Morton Place is named after Thomas Morton, one of the first to develop the land on what was then the western fringe of the town. Morton's inventions helped the local carpet industry but he is best remembered for his work as an astronomer. He built his observatory here in 1818 and constructed telescopes and a camera obscura. He made a telescope for Sir John Ross when he went to search for the north west passage. He was the first magistrate elected in Kilmarnock after the Reform Act of 1832. Early in the 20th century the observatory was used for weather forecasts.

Mossgiel Avenue

Mossgiel is the farm near Mauchline which was farmed by Robert Burns and his brother, Gilbert, from 1784.

Mount Pleasant

Mount Pleasant is an old name for a slight hill in Wellington Street. The old Kilmarnock Infirmary was built here in 1869.

Mountgean

Mountgean has gone by various names over the years. See the entry for Morris Street.

Kilmarnock Imfirmary was built on a hill known as Mount Pleasant.

Rosie Jackson outside her father's Nelson Street Shop in 1904.

Nailers Close

Nailers Close was a narrow path linking the Cross and Green Street. In 1808 it was the scene of a brutal murder, when a soldier was killed by a deserter. Although most of Nailers Close was removed in the 1850s for the construction of Duke Street some fragments of it remained into the 20th century.

Neephill

Neephill was a row of cottages for miners, situated on the road which went close by the Mount Estate, linking Dundonald Road and Irvine Road. Although most of the cottages were demolished in the 1930s, some survived into the 1950s.

Nelson Street

Nelson Street existed as an unnamed route long before it was named after Admiral Lord Nelson. The part close to the Timmer Brig was known as Swine Raw. Today Nelson Street continues to be narrow and crooked but it gives only a faint image of the former street.

Netherton

Netherton was once a minor village between Kilmarnock and Riccarton at Nethertonholm. The area was opened up in the 1760s by the building of what became Titchfield Street, Low and High Glencairn Streets and the Holm Square or Glencairn Square. Today East and West Netherton Streets are in this area. Towards the end of the 18th century the area was well known for weaving and carpet making. The Netherton was referred to by Burns in The Ordination.

New Farm

New Farm Loch is a major housing scheme on the eastern side of Kilmarnock. Construction of houses began there in the late 1960s, but the decision to develop this land for houses was taken at a meeting of Ayr County Council in March, 1952. The New Farm Loch was a popular venue for outdoor curling.

New Mill Road

When the town mill was moved from the Cross to what is now Scott Ellis in 1703, the route to it was given the name New Mill Road, but the route probably existed before that as part of the way from the Netherton to Struthers Steps at Crookedholm. Some of the houses here bear the date 1926.

New Raw

What became Boyd Street was originally Mountgean, then New Raw, presumably after houses were built for the first time, then it became Morris Street.

New Street

New Street was opened up in 1744 to improve access from Back Street and Soulis Street to the town Green and the river. At the start of the 19th century it was the best street in town, but by the end of the 19th century it was the narrowest street in Kilmarnock. It was only 15 feet wide. Rev David Landsborough said that at one time it was; 'delightfully sheltered from every cold or violent wind, and yet lying so nicely to the sun'. It ran from between Fore Street (now the Foregate) and Soulis Street to Clerks Lane. Today the site is occupied by the bus station.

This is New Street, when it was very old.

New Street, Riccarton

If Kilmarnock can have a new street why not Riccarton? The one in Riccarton was created out of Crompton Street in the middle of the 19th century. The last thatched cottage in Kilmarnock and Riccarton was in New Street. It was re-roofed in 1911. It was also the birthplace of 19th century singer, John Templeton.

New Mill Burn

The New Mill Burn was one of several burns and streams which ran through Kilmarnock. However, rather than make a feature of this, the local authority had this and other burns encased in a tunnel of concrete and buried. This one enters the River Irvine at Scott Ellis, near the New Mill.

Newton Walk

Newton Walk has nothing to do with the great scientist. The area known as Newton was owned by James Robertson and when it was built on, it became Robertson Place. In the 1970s the Robertson Place area was redeveloped and one of the names used was the old one of Newton Walk.

No Name Lane

When the town centre was being refurbished in the 1990s stones were put in place with names of each street, but one narrow close, linking King Street and Sandbed Street had no name, so the stone reads No Name Lanc, giving an impression that is now its name.

Northcraig Road

Northcraig Road takes its name from the North Craig reservoir to the north of Kilmarnock. Until about 1999-2000 the reservoir was remote from the town, but the steady growth of Kilmarnock has made it close to the built up area.

North Hamilton Street

One of several streets opened up or expanded between 1851 and 1879. This was formerly part of Great Hamilton Street. At the top of the street are the Cheeny Buildings with their white glazed bricks. The end building has a brick dated 1883 on it.

Nursery Avenue

Nursery Avenue was the route leading to Samson's Nursery and to what became known as the New Pit Nursery. Later, Nursery Avenue became the main depot for Western SMT buses.

Nursery Street

Nursery Street was the route leading to Netherton Nursery.

Nursery Terrace

Nursery Terrace was one of the Terraces off London Road. It takes its name from Tam Samson's nursery.

Ogilvie Place

Ogilvie Place is in New Farm Loch, along with streets with names presumably commemorating people named, Brodie, Erskine, Grant, Keith, Dunbar and Armstrong. But it is no longer clear who is commemorated in these streets. *See 'Clans'.*

Old Cast Lane

Old Cast Lane is the remains of a lane behind Titchfield Street. It may, at one time, have been part of a continuation of the Sandbed.

The cheeny buildings in North Hamilton Street.

The Old High Church, which dates from 1731.

Old High Church

The Old High dates from 1731, having been built to accommodate a growing population. The architecture is plain and the tower is a later addition to the building. In the kirkyard there are stones to John Wilson who printed the first edition of Burns poetry and established Ayrshire's first newspaper; Thomas Kennedy, founder of Glenfield and Kennedy; Thomas Morton, inventor, industrialist and amateur astronomer and John and William Tannock, artists.

Old Irvine Road

Formerly what is now Old Irvine Road was the only road from Kilmarnock to Irvine.

Old Mill road

Before the corn mill was moved from the Cross in 1703, the street leading to it was known as Mill Road. With the mill being moved to what is now Scott Ellis, the name became Old Mill Road and the road leading to the new mill became New Mill Road.

Oliphant Drive

Oliphant Drive commemorates Kilmarnock's connection with Burns in two ways. Rev. James Oliphant was an evangelical minister of the High Kirk in the time of Burns. He is featured in the poem The Ordination. Burns and his family also worked the farm known as Mount Oliphant until 1777.

Onthank

Onthank, now a major area of local authority houses, takes its name from the old Onthank Farm. The name may come from the fact that the ground was poor for farming and therefore 'unthankful'. This became corrupted as Onthank.

Orchard Street

Land from Orchard Street to Thomson Street was once a market garden of some note but in the 1870s houses began to be built there.

Paddy's Brae

After being modernised, Paddy's Brae became East George Street.

Paddy's Castle

Paddy's Castle was a three storey tenement block with four families on each floor. It was at the foot of Bentinck Street and was demolished in the 1930s.

Paddy's Close

Paddy's Close was off Soulis Street, and was said by Archibald Adamson in 1875 to be a cluster of houses that still retained a look of faded grandeur.

Park Lane

The origin the name of this now demolished street is obscure, but it may relate to early owners of Langlands House.

Park Street

As with Park Lane, the name may have come from a local property owner. Park Street was popularly known as the Gas Brae because the gas works were here.

Pathhead

Pathhead, also known as Rackhead, was the old name for what is now Fulton's Lane.

Pawn Lawn

Pawn Lawn was the name of an area of Low Glencairn Street close to which was Kilmarnock's only distillery. It takes it's name from a Pawnbroker's business.

Park Street was also known as the Gas Brae because the town's gas works were there.

Paxton Street

Paxton Street and the present day Paxton Place were both named after brewer George Paxton who owned the Richardland Brewery and Richardland House.

Peace and Plenty

Peace and Plenty was a row of miners' cottages a mile south of Riccarton on the Ayr Road. It was noted, at least in the 19th century, for the excellence of the tidy gardens, and was named after an old hostelry.

Peace Avenue

Peace Avenue is a short street of modern houses between Yorke Place and Irvine Road, with an ever-so politically correct name.

Peewit Toll

The Peewit Toll was at a crossroads on the route from Treeswoodhead Road out towards Craigie and Carnell.

Pentland Road

Pentland Road in Bellfield commemorates the Covenanters who were defeated at Pentland near Edinburgh in 1667. The assault on them was lead by General Tam Dalziel who for some time kept his headquarters in Kilmarnock. His brutality earned him the nickname of bloody Dalziel.

Picken Street

Picken Street in Riccarton may be named after Hugh Picken, a local businessman of the 19th century.

The Peace and Plenty, originally a miners' row.

This is Portland Road in the early years of the 20th century.

Pie Raw

Pie Raw was a group of houses close to Riccarton Bridge. The houses are supposed to have been built by a baker who made pies and the place was named in his honour. The houses, however, were subjected to periodic flooding. What was Pie Raw became Academy Street, but the old name persisted well into the 20th century.

Piersland

Piersland Park is a small recreation park, off London Road. It was opened in 1925 on land provided by the whiskey baron, Sir Alexander Walker, grandson of Johnnie Walker. Piersland Place was situated on land adjacent to Piersland Park. The name comes from the family home, Piersland in Troon which is now a hotel.

Pipe's Brae

Not much is known about Pipe's Brae, but it is mentioned in a Town Council minute of 1757, which refers to a dispute over a fence, 'on the side of the Town's ground opposite Pipe's Brae,' adjoining town Holm.

Porting Cross Place

Porting Cross Place is one of the late 1990s streets of the Southcraig. Beside it are streets named after Ayrshire towns and villages such as Ochiltree, Stewarton and Tarbolton. It is assumed that this street was named in error and that it was supposed to represent the village of Portencross.

Portland Road

Portland Road was named after the Duke of Portland. This street extended the western extremity of the town beyond Saint Marnock Street. Note that the first two houses beyond Holy Trinity Church are set back from the road. This is the point where the Kilmarnock and Troon Railway line came in when the original terminus was at the offices of Kilmarnock House. Portland Place is off Portland Road.

Portland Street as seen in a postcard of 1934.

Portland Gate

After decades of neglect the remnants of what was Portland Street has started to be redeveloped with shops, a restaurant and a night club, under the new name of Portland Gate. A major development here was opened towards the end of 2000.

Portland Street

Portland Street was opened up after King Street and was developed in the first two decades of the 19th century. It became one of the main commercial streets of the town, and it opened up the land to the North of the Cross. It was named after the Duke of Portland, local landowner. The building now used as Mason Murphy's furniture shop was the George Hotel and it was built on the site of Sandy Patrick's pub which was often frequented by Robert Burns. Here, too, was the original site for the Kilmarnock Bowling Club, established in 1740. Portland Street continues beyond the railway arches and here is the West High Church. As this book was being written the future of this church building was uncertain. The building has a war memorial on an external wall.

Portland Terrace

Portland Terrace is a row of houses in Portland Road.

Pottery Place

Pottery Place is one of several streets built on land of one of Kilmarnock's extensive J & M Craig pottery works. The company were major producers of bricks and pottery and stone ornaments such as the lions in Dean and Kay Parks.

Princes Street

Princes Street was close to King Street and Queen Street. It was here that the Kilmarnock Co-op was founded. The Co-op went on to dominate retailing in Kilmarnock for most of the first half of the 20th century. Also in Princes Street was a building with a lion and a unicorn carved into the stone work.

Queen Street

Queen Street was named after Queen Victoria. It is at right angles to King Street and was once of much greater importance than it is today.

Queen's Drive

Queen's Drive is named after Queen Victoria. The road has also gone by the name of Bellfield Drive. During the 1990's, a relaxation of local planning policy allowed the rapid development of this area for commercial and leisure use. Today there are car showrooms, a retail park, supermarket, cinema and restaurants. At the Kilmarnock end of the road is Victoria Bridge, over the River Irvine.

Rackhead

Rackhead was also known as Pathhead. It was possibly named by curlers who used the area, a rack being their name for the path used by the curling stone. Today it is Fulton's Lane.

Railway Station

Kilmarnock's railway station of today dates largely from the 1870s. It was built by the Glasgow and South Western Railway and if you look at the roof brackets on the platforms, you will be able to pick out the letters G&SWR which are intertwined to form a pattern.

Rankin Court

Rankin Court in New Farm Loch may be named after an enterprising family from Kilmarnock. William Rankin, and later his son, David, ran the post office in Kilmarnock for most of the 19th century. They also had other business interests, notably Rankin and Borland, a chemists which lasted into the second half of the 20th century.

Rathlin Avenue

Rathlin Avenue is named after Rathlin Island off the coast of Antrim. Robert the Bruce fled to Rathlin after defeat in battle but legend says that it was while he was at Rathlin he was inspired by a spider not to give up the struggle for Scottish independence.

Reeky Lands

Reeky Lands was the name given to a farm which existed on what is now Queen's Drive about the middle of the 19th century. There was also a Reeky Laun in New Street, Riccarton.

Regent Street

Regent Street was formed around 1570 and was probably named after Regent Moray of Scotland who was assassinated in that year. It formed part of the Cross area. Part of the street was demolished in the late 1850s to make way for a new street linking the Cross and London Road. Regent Street remained an important part of the town centre until demolition in the 1970s.

Regent Street in the 1920s.

Rennie Street

Rennie Street, an early 20th century residential street of villas, is named after James Rennie, a Kilmarnock magistrate.

Riccarton Bridge

The River Irvine marked the boundary not just between Kilmarnock and Irvine but between Cunninghame and Kyle. The old Riccarton bridge was built in 1726. The date is etched on to it but today it is hard to read. The stepping stones this bridge replaces were still being marked on local maps of the mid-19th century. The Riccarton Bridge, carrying the main road dates from the 1840s.

Riccarton Castle

Nothing remains of Riccarton Castle which is thought to have stood on or close to the Moat hill on which the present Riccarton Church is built. The castle was the property of the Wallace family and they subsequently moved to Craigie. A

charter of 1165 gave lands at Riccarton to Richard Wallace, believed to be the grandfather of Scotland's greatest hero. From that Richard comes the name Richardland, which is still in use, and Richardtown, which we know today as Riccarton.

Richardland Road

Richardland is supposed to take its name from Richard Wallace, the patriach of the Wallace family who is also remembered in the name Riccarton. This road, originally Mill Dykes led to Richardland House and the Brewery of George Paxton.

River Irvine

The River Irvine is one of the two rivers flowing through the town and although greater than the Kilmarnock Water the River Irvine played a lesser part in the early development of the town. The river rises in the moors beyond Darvel and flows into the sea at Irvine. The main tributaries are Kilmarnock Water and the Cessnock.

Riverbank Place

As the name suggests this was on the banks of the River Irvine.

Robertson Mount

Robertson Mount is an old name for the hill in Kilmarnock at the junction of what was Robertson Place and Clark Street, It is now occupied by Lillymount House.

Robertson Place

In 1824 the Kilmarnock Building Company was formed. Members each paid an entry fee and a monthly subscription to allow the building of houses. The first street they built was Robertson Place. It was named after James Robertson on whose land it was built. The original name was the Newton. Robertson Place was demolished and rebuilt in the 1960s and the old name was brought back in Newton Walk after redevelopment of the adjacent area in the 1970s.

Rugby Park

When Kilmarnock Football Club was founded it was a general sports club with a wide variety of interests and the playingfield was known as Rugby Park. Gradually the interest was concentrated on soccer, but the Rugby Park name was retained even when the ground was relocated in 1899. Rugby Road leads to Rugby Park from South Hamilton Street and Rugby Crescent is also adjacent to the ground.

Rowallan

It is not clear how Rowallan Castle acquired its name, but the castle has now lent its name to a drive, a creamery, a business park and at one time a school.

Rumford Place

Rumford Place is an old version of the more Anglicised Romeford, a river crossing at Old Rome, Gatehead.

The Toll House, Riccarton

Riccarton has twa brigs and the tollhouse was between them.

Rumpy

The farm of Rumpy was at the southern end of the Wards Park, now Howard Park.

Saint Andrew

Part of Saint Andrew Street is very old and the line of it appears on a map of 1783. At this time it was known as the back road. There was at one time a quarry in front of St Andrew's Church. In 1816 spoil from levelling part of Gallion Brae was poured into the quarry hole. The Blackwood family started spinning yarn in St Andrew Street in 1791 and are still in the town today. After redevelopment in the 1970s the street was split into two distinct parts with completely separate entry points. Saint Andrew Terrace is a row of modern houses off Saint Andrew Street very close to what was Gallion Brae. Saint Andrew Lane linked Saint Andrew Street and Kirktonholm Street.

The kirkyard around the church contains the graves of several notable people including Johnnie Walker who founded the vast whisky empire and Alexander Geddes who was governor of the town jail for many years.

Saint Marnock Place

Saint Marnock Place is a short Street linking Saint Marnock Street and Nelson Street. Near here was Ha's Well, which was said to produce the best water for adding to whisky.

Saint Marnock Street

Saint Marnock Street is named after the supposed founder of Kilmarnock. Kilmarnock House was in here, though it pre-dated any street. The site of Kilmarnock House is now a car park. The building was the town house of the Boyds and their main residence after the fire at

Saint Marnock Street, showing the Courthouse and part of Kilmarnock House.

Dean Castle in 1735. Saint Marnock Street today has several interesting buildings. The office of the procurator fiscal is the former Sheriff Court House, which dates from 1852. This was built on land at the corner of Saint Marnock Street and Bank Street. The offices of Kilmarnock House, in Bank Street, served as the passenger terminus and ticket office of the Kilmarnock and Troon Railway as early as 1812. A plaque on the former court house building marks this. The new court house on the corner with Dundonald Road was opened in 1987. Saint Marnock Street also houses the area Police Headquarters and St Marnock Street Church, which was built in 1836. Saint Marnock Place is a minor road leading on to Saint Marnock Street from Nelson Street.

Saint Marnock Street Bridge

Before Saint Marnock Street was opened up there was a wooden footbridge here and a ford a little further down stream. Perhaps when the stone bridge was built the bridge at Nelson Street was given the name Timmer Brig, a timber bridge as opposed to the stone bridge.

Samson Avenue

Samson Avenue is a street of council housing built on land once cultivated by Samson's, the firm founded by Tam Samson, who was a friend of Robert Burns. In the days when Kilmarnock had its own town council it was the practice to put two lamps outside the home of the provost and leave one there after a new provost had been appointed. One of the last provosts of Kilmarnock Town Council was Annie Mackie and the lamp is still outside her former home in Samson Avenue.

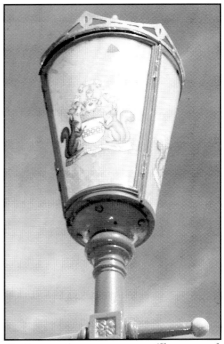

In Samson Avenue you can still see one of the old Provost's lamps.

Sandbed Bridge

On the site of the earliest bridge over the Kilmarnock Water, the present bridge links Cheapside and Bank Street with the Sandbed, or Sandbed Street. It was described by Timothy Pont about 1612 as 'a faire stone bridge', but in 1658 another traveller, Richard Franck said it was 'wretchedly ancient'. The bridge was renewed at about this time and was substantially repaired in 1753 following flood damage. The present one was built in 1762. Until the Fleshmarket Bridge was built in 1770 the town market was held on the Sandbed Bridge.

Sandbed Lane

Sandbed Lane links the Sandbed to King Street. At one time there was an old water pump at the foot of Sandbed Lane.

Sandbed Street

Sandbed Street is sometimes referred to as the Sandbed. It is one of the very early streets of the town. Before King Street was built in 1804 the Sandbed was the main route through Kilmarnock to the south. In former times stones and sand from the river alongside this street was taken for building. In 1856 it was reported that old folk still living in the town could remember when strings of pack horses could be seen in the Sandbed on their way to Glasgow. A weir in the river near here was removed at the end of the 19th century.

Sands' Close

Sands Close was just off Titchfield Street almost opposite the opening to Old Cast Lane. It was removed about the end of the 19th century.

Sanny Brig

The Sanny Brig, or Sandy Bridge is a name sometimes used for the bridge which takes the railway over the River Irvine between Kilmarnock and Crookedholm.

Scott-Ellis

The Scott Ellis Playing Fields were given to Kilmarnock by Lord Howard de Walden in 1939. Although used for various sports and for visiting circuses and fairs, the land has never been fully developed for such events.

Scott Road

Scott Road is named after Henrietta Scott, a wealthy land owner. Council houses were first built here in the 1920s.

Seaford Street

Seaford Street was named after Charles Augustus, 2nd Baron Seaford, 6th Baron Howard de Walden.

Shanks Court

Shanks Court is a reminder of Kilmarnock's industrial past. Houses here are built on land once occupied by J & M Craig who were major producers of bricks and pottery. The company eventually became part of Shanks.

Shanter Place

Shanter Place is named after Tam o' Shanter, hero of one of Burns' best loved poems.

Sheeling Hill

Sheeling Hill, or Shieling Hill was the hill on which the railway station was built. It was at one time used to shiel the corn, that is separate the grain and husk using the wind. At that time the town's corn mill stood at the cross and was driven by water from a lade which took water from Kilmarnock Water.

Shuttle Street

Shuttle Street was one of several streets opened in the period immediately after the Improvement Act of 1804. It is now called Douglas Street and was the birthplace of Alexander Smith.

Smiddie Raw

Smiddie Raw, sometimes recorded as Smiddieraw, was one of the very early streets of the town, dating from around the 17th century. It later became Back Street.

Soulis Street

Soulis Street occupies one of the oldest parts of Kilmarnock. Lord Soulis is an enigmatic figure in Kilmarnock's history. One version is that the family owned Dean Castle before the Boyds, another that he was killed by the Boyds in battle. In the middle of the 18th century Soulis Street was one of the preferred streets for the homes of the wealthy, but houses were small and badly ventilated. One resident of the street was Gavin Turnbull a contemporary of Burns and a poet whose work Burns admired. Turnbull eventually went to America. Soulis Street has a memorial pillar and a plaque to Lord Soulis but it sheds little light on why he should be commemorated. The original Soulis Cross, presumably a market cross, is said to have been dated 1444. It was removed in 1825. Soulis Street also has an entrance to the High Kirk.

Souter Drive

Souter is an old name for a shoemaker. Souter Drive is close to Oliphant Drive, Cotter Drive and Shanter Place, all names associated with Robert Burns. In the poem Tam o' Shanter, Tam's best pal is Souter Johnnie: His ancient, trusty, drouthy cronie.

South Craig

South Craig was a farm in the vicinity of Onthank. Today it has given its name to a major housing and commercial development to the north of Kilmarnock.

South Dean Road

South Dean Road takes its name from the one time South Dean Farm.

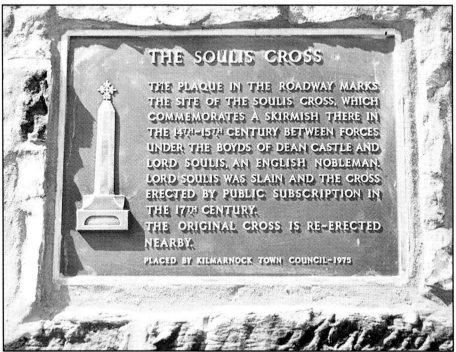

Soulis Street presents a confused tale for the historian.

The house at the corner of South Hamilton Street and South Hamilton Place was once the Nursing Association Home

South Hamilton Street

One of several streets opened up or expanded between 1851 and 1879. Great Hamilton Street was split into North and South Hamilton Street. South Hamilton Place is a small area of houses off South Hamilton Street. The house on the corner between the two was a nurses' home.

Southhook Road

Southhook Road is named after the once extensive Southhook pit and pottery works. From the late 19th century until the 1970s, they made bricks, particularly glazed bricks, sanitary ware and other pottery items.

South Knockinlaw

A map of the town as it was in 1783 shows South Knockinlaw as a farm to the north of the town and well away from any built up developments. Today Knockinlaw is used as a general area of the town.

Sparrow Plantation

Sparrow Plantation is a modern housing development off London Road including Osprey Drive, Finch Place, Bunting Place and Sparrow Gardens.

Spittalhill

Spittalhill is on the southern edge of Kilmarnock at the southern end of the bypass. At one time there was a hospital in the area.

Star Inn Close

The Star Inn Close was part of Greenfoot, which later became Waterloo Street. It was here that John Wilson printed the first edition of the works of Robert Burns in 1786. Although best remembered for his association with Burns, Wilson is worth remembering on his own merit. He was a magistrate and a successful businessman. He established the first press in Kilmarnock and later produced Ayrshire's first newspaper. Today his statue stands at the Cross alongside that of Robert Burns.

Stevenson Street

There is uncertainty about the origin of the name Stevenson Street, but it could be named after Thomas Stevenson who founded the Kilmarnock Standard.

Stirling Avenue

Stirling Avenue and Stirling Crescent off the Irvine Road are probably named after James and Patrick Stirling, locomotive designers who came from Kilmarnock.

Stoneyhill Avenue

A map drawn in 1832 shows a building named Stoneyhill just about where Stoneyhill Avenue is today. Council houses began to be built here in the 1930s.

Strand Street

Strand Street or the Strand was one of the very early streets of the town, dating from at least the 17th century. It may take its name from the Strand burn. Around 1700 the Strand was the only street of importance in Kilmarnock and was the first street in the town to be paved. By the middle of the 18th century it was still the preferred street for the homes of the merchants, but houses were small and badly ventilated. The street ran from Cheapside, near the Cross to the Strandhead Toll close to what was called Hawket Park in what is now Hill Street.

Strawberrybank Road

Strawberrybank Road was formerly Willie Mair's Brae, occasionally referred to as Willie Muir's Brae. It is close to the Kay Park.

This is an artist's impression of what the Star Inn Close looked like about the time Burns came to Kilmarnock to have his works printed.

Part of Nelson Street near the Timmer Brig known as Swine Raw because some folk kept pigs here.

Struan Villas

Struan Villas forms part of Portland Road.

Struthers Steps

The Struthers Steps was a series of stepping stones across the River Irvine close to Struthers Farm, near Crookedholm. By 1880 the steps were almost worn away and the Reid Bridge was built to replace them. The name, however, persisted.

Sturrock Street

Kilmarnock Provost Peter Sturrock gave his name to Sturrock Street in the town centre. The burgh police station and court house was built here in 1898 and served until the 1970s. Peter Sturrock took a keen interest in all that was happening in Kilmarnock and was a keen Burns scholar who served on the committee of the Burns Federation.

Swine Raw

A group of houses known as Swine Raw existed into the 20th century in Nelson Street close to where the Timmer Brig crosses the river. The name is supposed to have been given to the row when the people there kept pigs. Some of the buildings remained into the 20th century.

Symington Terrace

Some of the even numbered red sandstone tenements in Arbuckle Street were known as Symington Terrace. It was probably named after Rev John Symington who was minister of King Street church from 1847 until his death in 1871.

Tam's Loup

Tam's Loup is a rock at a bend in the Kilmarnock Water close to Townholm. The pool here was once a popular place for swimming. It is an old name but who Tam was is not known.

Tankerha' Brae

Tankerha' Brae or Tankardha Brae is a steep rise up the hill on the banks of the Kilmarnock Water. Maps and directories can't agree on the spelling but was possibly originally Tankerhaugh, a haugh being land on the outside curve of the river. At one time factories clung precariously to the hillside here and part of the ground was known as Hatter's Land because hats were made here.

Tannock Street

Tannock Street was named after James Tannock a local artist of some note who lived in Grange Street.

The Place

The Place was a popular name for Kilmarnock House, which was in what is now Saint Marnock Street. The site of the house is now a car park.

Thirdpart Street

Thirdpart Street is named after the farm which, on some old maps, is Third Part. It was close to the bank of the River Irvine between Kilmarnock and Gatehead.

Thomson Street

Thomson Street was probably named after James Thomson, a local geologist.

Timmer Land

Part of Boyd Street was frequently referred to as Timmer Land. In Rambles Round Kilmarnock (1875) Archibald Adams said that in this place a man named Wallace had lately 'dashed the brains of a little child out against the hearthstone'.

This sketch from an old Kilmarnock Standard Annual shows an atrist's impression of Titchfield Avenue.

Timmer Brig

The footbridge over the Kilmarnock Water at Nelson Street has long been called the Timmer Brig, but it is not clear just when a footbridge was first in place here. There seems to have been one as early as 1762. There was a timber footbridge at what is now Saint Marnock Street before a stone bridge replaced both footbridge and ford. The Timmer Brig linking the Sandbed to Nelson Street was washed away by the flood of 1852, and the replacement was built about two feet higher. The present Timmer Brig replaced the earlier one in 1991.

Titchfield Street

The route from Kilmarnock to the Netherton was sometimes referred to as Titchfield Avenue before the street was straightened and widened in 1865 to become Titchfield Street. This new wide and straight road provided a good road from the Cross to Netherton and on to Riccarton. It was named after the Marquis of Titchfield, son of the Duke of Portland. In the early years buildings were mostly single storey and with a thatched roof. Today's prominent buildings include the former cinema, originally built as a theatre and now a shopping arcade. There is also the Galleon Leisure Centre, built on the site of the Saxone shoe factory. A stone showing a cordwainer at work was a feature of the Saxone building. It was preserved when the building was demolished and is now in the Galleon. On the opposite side of the street from the Galleon, there is a car park which was the site of the former swimming baths. This was the first indoor swimming pool in Britain to have a wave making machine. Titchfield Street post office is the oldest sub post office in Kilmarnock on its original site. The post box outside is Victorian and appears to be unique in Scotland in having been a Victorian box with a stamp vending machine. The machine was removed in 1971, but an enamel plate giving instructions is still attached to the box. A few buildings in Titchfield Street still have tram rosettes on them. The tram cars were used here from 1904 to 1926. Some relics have been found in Titchfield Street, such as an ancient funeral urn.

This is Titchfield Street in the early years of the 20th century.

Todrig Drive

Todrig Drive close to Caprington Golf Course takes its name from Todrig Farm, near Gatehead. The farm was the birthplace in 1805 of Johnnie Walker, the founder of the vast whisky empire.

Townend

At the close of the 18th century the edge of the town, or Townend was around the area of Woodstock Street, Townend House, was the home of James Gregory, the town registrar.

Townhead

Much of the built up area to the north of the Cross became known as Townhead in the 18th century. The Townhead Bridge was built in 1770. Much of the area was redeveloped in 1869 with one side of the street leading to Townholm being removed to widen the road.

Townholm

Named the Town Holm to distinguish it from The Holm, near Riccarton, this area had very few buildings until the second quarter of the 18th century. Before that it was cultivated with cornfields. The town's first foundry was at Townholm. In the 20th century it became a housing area with council houses built here in the 1920s, but latterly it was terribly run down. It became such an area of neglect that the houses were eventually demolished.

Trees

A group of streets in the Grange estate is named after trees including Ash, Beech, Willow, Chestnut, Lilac, Larch and Lime.

Treesbank

Treesbank House was a mansion off the Ayr Road at the southern extremity of Kilmarnock. It was originally built by Sir Hugh Campbell of Cessnock and given to his son as a wedding present in 1672. It was substantially rebuilt 200 years later and again by BMK in 1936.

Treeswoodhead Road

Treeswoodhead Road used to be a country road but now marks the boundary between Shortlees and Riccarton.

Turnberry Drive

Turnberry Drive takes its name from Turnberry Castle on the Ayrshire coast. Turnberry was the birthplace of King Robert the Bruce who lead Scotland to independence at the battle of Bannockburn in 1314.

Turner Place

Frederick and Joseph Turner were factors to the Duke of Portland. They lived at the Dean but later moved to Cessnock Castle. Turner Place, a row of single storey cottages, was built for retired estate workers and named after them.

Umberley Road

Umberley Road is just off the Ayr Road at the edge of Kilmarnock. It takes its name from what was Umberley House, sometimes referred to as Umberlie House. When Caprington Golf Course was opened in the first decade of the 20th century, Umberley House was used as the clubhouse.

Underwood Place

Underwood Place in Shortlees takes its name from Underwood House near Symington.

Union Street

Union Street was opened in October, 1860 by the Provost with suitable civic ceremony and even a volley of shots being fired. It was built to unite High Street and Wellington Street.

Viaduct

The railway viaduct dominates the centre of Kilmarnock. The massive structure of 23 arches was built in 1848 to take the Glasgow to Kilmarnock railway on to Dumfries and Carlisle. A chisel mark on the bridge near what was Ladeside is supposed to mark the level of the 1852 flood, but I have never found it.

Victoria Bridge

Victoria Bridge crosses the River Irvine and links Welbeck Street with the Queen's Drive. The bridge was rebuilt in 1972.

Victoria Place

Victoria Place was a name occasionally used in the 19th century for an area between the Sandbed Bridge and the Cross. A map of 1857 shows it as the single storey building facing on to King Street where the river flows below.

Victoria Terrace

Victoria Terrace was a row of tenement houses on the banks of the River Irvine close to Victoria Bridge which linked Welbeck Street and the Queen's Drive.

Vorlich Place

Ben Vorlich in Perthshire is 3,225 feet high and on a clear day is visible from the highest points around Kilmarnock.

The railway viaduct is now a backdrop to the core of Kilmarnock.

Wallace Street

Wallace Street is a residential street close to Howard Park. It is no longer clear whether this street commemorates Sir William Wallace, the hero of the war of independence, or William Wallace who founded a whisky empire in Kilmarnock.

Wallace View

Wallace View in Riccarton commemorates the association of the Wallace family with Riccarton, and in particular, Sir William Wallace who laid the groundwork for the independence struggle. There are many local tales about Wallace's youth and recent evidence supports the view that Wallace was probably born in Ayrshire. The Wallace family held a charter for land at Riccarton from 1165.

Wallhill

There was a farm by the name of Wallhill in Riccarton. It was on the Kilmarnock side of the church and it bordered Old Street. Here, too, was Wallhill Road, probably the original road from Riccarton into Kilmarnock.

Wardneuk

Wardneuk is now a general area of Kilmarnock, and like several other areas takes its name from a farm which used to occupy land now used for housing. At the time when the town's mill was at the Cross, the occupants of Wardneuk farm were the Rankin family, who later ran the post office for most of the 19th century and founded Rankin and Borland, which was a major chemist's shop in Kilmarnock until the middle of the 20th century.

Wards Park

In 1749 the ancient Wards Park and Barbados Green were sold to the Earl of Glencairn, by the town council. He was the superior of the burgh at that time. The Wards Park is now part of Howard Park.

Wards Place

The houses face on to Howard Park and were built on land that was once part of the Wards Park.

War Memorial

Kilmarnock's War Memorial was built in the form of a temple and dedicated in 1927. It contains plaques naming the local men who died 'for king and country' in two world wars and a fine statue of The Victor by local sculptor David McGill. Other war memorials in the town include plaques in the Post Office in John Finnie Street, and in Kilmarnock Academy, on the outside wall of the West High Church in Portland Street and in the Kilmarnock Cemetery in Grassyards Road.

Water Lane

Water Lane is one of several short and narrow lanes which lead from King Street to the Sandbed.

Waterloo Street

Waterloo Street was a narrow lane until it was reshaped into a street in 1752. At that time it was called Greenfoot as it led from the Cross to the town Green. Many local men fought in the battle of Waterloo in 1815 and the street was renamed in commemoration of the battle and subsequent liberation of Europe. John Wilson established his printing press here and in 1786 printed the Kilmarnock Edition of the poems of Robert Burns. He later moved to Ayr and established Ayrshire's first newspaper. In 1875, Archibald Adamson described the houses in Waterloo Street as 'dingy and old fashioned'. Like so much of Kilmarnock's heritage, Waterloo Street was demolished in the 1970s and the site is now the Burns Shopping Centre. A plaque marking the site of Wilson's printworks was preserved and is now in the shopping centre. Waterloo Street Post Office retained its name when it moved to the Foregate in 1974.

Waterside Street

Waterside Street or Waterside is on the banks of the Kilmarnock Water between the Howard Park and Saint Marnock Street. In former times it was much larger, stretching from Kilmarnock House to Barbadoes Green (Howard Park). In 1875 it was described as 'a row of old fashioned houses' by Archibald Adamson.

Welbeck Street

Welbeck Street is named after Welbeck Abbey, Nottinghamshire, seat of the Dukes of Portland. The family owned much of the land around Kilmarnock and various streets are named after their connections.

Wellington Street

Wellington Street was opened up in 1812 and named after the hero of the battle of Waterloo. Here on a hill called Mount Pleasant Kilmarnock Infirmary was built and served the town for 100 years. One of the two Kay schools was built in Wellington Street. Here, too was Galahill, originally a mansion, it became a girls' hostel in the 1940s. Today at the top end of Wellington Street a block of council built homes sports an old sandstone coat of arms, presumably from a building that once occupied that site.

West George Street just after the Second World War.

Western Road

Western Road was originally conceived as a western by-pass road to help divert traffic away from the town centre, but it was only ever partially built and today has houses built on both sides. Just off Western Road is Western Place.

West Fullarton Street

As with Fullarton Street, this was named after the old Fullarton estate in Troon, which was purchased by the Duke of Portland and used as his main Scottish residence.

West George Street

West George Street was named after George III and linked John Finnie Street with Portland Street. West George Street Lane was a lane leading off West George Street.

West Langlands Street

West Langlands Street is named after the Langlands House and estate. It runs from the top of John Finnie Street until it merges into Bonnyton Road. Here is the telephone exchange with 1963 on a plate in the building. Here too are the works of Hunslet Barclay, the last locomotive builders in Scotland. An unusual railway line crosses the road to link the buildings of the works. It is designed to take locomotives of two different gauges. A room on the top floor of the Building on the corner of West Langlands Street and North Hamilton Street was used by Andrew Barclay for astronomical observations. It has large windows on three sides. Barclay built his own telescopes in the works here.

Westmoor Nursery

The Westmoor Nursery was one of many nurseries now entirely within the built up area of Kilmarnock. This one took up most of the land between Dundonald Road and the railway line from just before Point House. On the other side of Dundonald Road, the Holmes Nursery filled a large triangle between Dundonald Road and Holmes Road.

West Netherton Street

Netherton was at one time a small collection of houses between Kilmarnock and Riccarton.

West Shaw Street

West Shaw Street was originally known as The Loan, West and East Shaw Streets were renamed in honour of Sir James Shaw from Riccarton who became Lord Mayor of London. The bridge over the Kilmarnock Water which links West Shaw Street to McClelland Drive was built by the local railway engineers Grant, Ritchie & Co., in 1888. Three plaques tell of its construction, opening and subsequent reconstruction. There used to be a spring at West Shaw Street which has a good reputation for making tea.

The West Shaw Street Bridge has various plaques to tell of its building and rebuilding.

Whatriggs Road

The line of Whatriggs Road existed before the Bellfield area was developed for housing in the 1950s and 1960s. It was the road that lead to Whatriggs Farm. On most maps, even in the 20th century, this farm is noted as Wheatriggs.

Whins, The

Part of the Scott Ellis Playing Fields was known as The Whins, at least up until the early 1970s, because of the profusion of whin, or gorse, growing there.

William Street

William Street was probably named after William Boyd, Earl of Kilmarnock. It did not exist until the 1890s.

Willie Mair's Brae

Willie Mair's Brae is sometimes referred to a Willie Muir's Brae. Until 1838 the road went up the hill from Townhead Bridge and by Strawberry Bank House. The brae was cut and the route substantially improved in 1838. It was named after William Muir, local landlord and has also been known as Muir's Brae Road and Muir's Bank.

Willie Ross Place

Willie Ross Place is named after William Ross who was (Westminster) MP for Kilmarnock from 1946 to 1979 and served two terms as Secretary of State for Scotland. He was also Kilmarnock's longest serving MP.

Willock Street

There is some doubt about the origin of the name Willock Street in Riccarton, but it probably relates to a John Willock who was a respected parish councillor in Riccarton in the 19th century.

Winton Place

Winton Place is part of Dundonald Road, from John Finnie Street to about Howard Street. It gave its name to Winton Place Church, which was established by the majority group who split from Clerk's Lane Church. At Winton Place Church, note that the ornamental toppings to the stone and metal gateposts match each other. The last stone gatepost before Howard Street once had 'Winton Place' etched on it but time and weather have badly eroded the name and only part of it is now visible.

Witch Knowe

Witchknowe Road in Riccarton takes its name from the WitchKnowe, an ancient name for a hill in the area. In 1832, the hill marked the southern boundary of Kilmarnock. Witchknowe Road and Witchknowe Avenue were developed for council housing in the 1930s. No historical connection with supposed witches has been found.

Witch Road

Formerly known as Witch Street, Witch Road was the route of the road, which linked the Kilmaurs Road to the Dean Street, and therefore the route to Glasgow. It is marked on some early maps but is not named. Until 1820 it was a narrow cow path, but new buildings went up in the 1830s and 1840s. Today nearly all the houses here date from the 1970s and 1980s. There is no evidence for a connection with witches as is claimed by some writers.

Woodstock

Woodstock Street and Woodstock Place are named after Viscount Woodstock, the first Earl of Portland. Part of Woodstock Street is sometimes referred to as West Woodstock Street and part is also known as Grange Place. Together they run from John Finnie Street to Fullarton Street.

Yardside Place

The farm of Yardside is said to have been built on the site of Riccarton Castle, once home to the Wallace family. In 1875, Archibald Adamson noted that some stately trees were all that remained of the Castle and its estate. An earlier castle at Riccarton may have once existed on the hill on which Riccarton Church is built now.

Yorke Place

Yorke Place is just off Bonnyton Road and runs along side it. It is named after Winifred Anna Dallas-Yorke, who married the Duke of Portland in 1889.

The Kilmarnock War Memorial is in Elmbank Drive. In it is this statue of The Victor, with head bowed in contemplation of the cost of the war.

Woodstock Street, looking to the Grange Church.

Bibliography

Autobiographical Reminiscences, James Paterson, Maurice Ogle, 1871.

Contributions to Local History, David Landsborough; The Kilmarnock Standard, 1879.

History of Kilmarnock, Archibald McKay and William Findlay; Kilmarnock Standard, (5th edition).

Kilmarnock, James A Mackay; Alloway Publishing, Darvel, 1992.

Kilmarnock street and trades directories; Dick Institute.

Kilmarnock Standard; and the *Kilmarnock Standard Annual,* Scottish & Universal Newspapers Ltd.

Maps of Kilmarnock 1792-1992, James E Knox, Kilmarnock and District History Group, 1992.

Newsletters of the Kilmarnock and District History Group.

Old Kilmarnock, James Walker; Arthur Guthrie & Sons, 1895.

Pictorial History of Kilmarnock, John Malkin; Alloway Publishing, Darvel, 1989.

Rambles Round Kilmarnock, Archibald Adamson, Kilmarnock Standard, 1875.

Sketches of Old Kilmarnock, Thomas Smellie; 1898.

Trip Round the World, Hugh Lauder; Dunlop and Drennan, 1896.